Hiram Pitt Bennet
Pioneer, Frontier Lawyer, Politician

Editor
Liston E. Leyendecker

Co-editors
Conrad Woodall
Holley R. Lange
Susan L. Hoskinson

Monograph 2
1988

COLORADO
HISTORICAL
SOCIETY

D1457236

*Emma Richardson Cherry in 1891 courtesy
of Geoffrey C. Bennet.*

Essays and Monographs in Colorado History

Editor
David N. Wetzel

Consulting Editor
Judith L. Gamble

Art Director
José Aguayo

Secretary
Mary Winnell

The Colorado Historical Society periodically publishes *Essays and Monographs in Colorado History* (ISSN 0731-2474) to provide a flexible scholarly forum for well-written, documented manuscripts on the history of Colorado and the Rocky Mountain West. Its twofold structure is designed to accommodate article-length manuscripts in the traditional journal style and longer, book-length works which appear as separate monographs within the series. Brief scholarly notes and comments are also welcomed. Volumes of *Essays*, which are now numbered consecutively, will include a comprehensive five-year index. Monographs carry their own number series and each is individually indexed.

As always, the Colorado Historical Society encourages unsolicited submissions. The publications of the Society generally follow the principles and conventions of the *Chicago Manual of Style,* and an author's guide is available on request. Manuscripts and queries should be addressed to: Publications Office, Colorado Historical Society, 1300 Broadway, Denver, CO 80203. The Colorado Historical Society disclaims responsibility for statements of fact or opinion made by contributors.

CONTENTS

ACKNOWLEDGMENTS

PARTICIPANTS in this project were members of a seminar in state and local history offered at Colorado State University during spring semester 1987. Basically the work entailed identification of names and verification of activities mentioned and described by Hiram Pitt Bennet in his memoirs.

The editors wish to extend their sincerest and warmest thanks to Diane Cole, James Harris, Ann Hilfinger, Ramona Hutchinson, Halcyon LaPoint, and Matthew Larson for their research assistance, expertise, and imagination, which contributed immensely to this endeavor in its early stages.

The sources of information used to verify Bennet's statements were located in the following repositories: Glenwood Public Library, Glenwood, Iowa; Morgan Library, Colorado State University; Norlin Library, University of Colorado–Boulder; Stephen H. Hart Library, Colorado Historical Society; Western History Department, Denver Public Library; Manuscript Division, State Historical Society of Wisconsin; University of Wisconsin–Madison; Colorado State Archives and Records Service; Office of the Clerk and Recorder, Garfield County, Colorado; and Office of the Recorder, Mills County, Iowa. Our heartfelt thanks go out to the staffs of all these institutions for their assistance and cooperation during this project.

Introduction
By Liston E. Leyendecker

IN 1986 Charlotte Waters of Denver brought to the Colorado Historical Society a typewritten transcript of the memoirs of her great-grandfather, Hiram Pitt Bennet, dictated in the months before his death in 1914 to his son, Robert Ames Bennet. It became immediately apparent that, unlike many pioneer reminiscences, these captured the spirit not only of early Colorado but of the entire American West during the middle years of the nineteenth century. Over his lifetime Bennet traveled from Maine to California, lived on the edge of one geographical frontier after another, sat in the company of America's greatest leaders during times of national crisis, and observed in simple detail the events, manners, and character of the country he so frequently traveled.

The greater part of the transcript, we found, was not confined to Colorado at all. In addition to his boyhood experiences in Ohio and Missouri and early forays into legal work and public life in Iowa and Nebraska, Bennet's account included descriptions of western life in general, including riverboat travel on the Mississippi, stage travel across the Nevada desert, and railroad travel at its very inception.

Here, then, was a chronicle of an age, not simply a new addition to the body of extant memoirs about the Pikes Peak gold rush or early life in Denver. Yet even in his account of these, Bennet's large role in the establishment of law and order in the territory and public spirited efforts on behalf of the struggling young settlement of Denver told an important tale of civilization building on the frontier. While Bennet never became a member of the inner circle of noted pioneers that included William N. Byers, Jerome B. Chaffee, and John Evans, his signature appeared alongside theirs on many occasions. More important, his civic, legal, and political activities led to his election as Colorado's first territorial delegate to Congress in 1861, a position he held through two terms.

As valuable and informative as we found it, however, this transcript nevertheless posed certain problems on first reading. The major difficulty lay in verifying its authenticity. For one thing, Bennet's descendants possessed only a carbon copy of the now-missing original typescript, which may have borne changes or corrections in Bennet's own hand or, even more important, Bennet's signature along with those of witnesses and a notary seal.[1] Another problem was that Robert Ames Bennet was a well-known early twentieth-century novelist, and it was possible that this was a fictionalized version of his father's career which he planned to use as the basis for a novel.

The task of authenticating the piece made it a prime candidate for examination by students enrolled in a graduate seminar on state and local history at Colorado State University during the spring of 1987. These scholars' efforts soon began to verify much of Bennet's story as they researched records in Colorado, Iowa, and Nebraska along with historical accounts of those states. Since funding was not available for travel to Maine, Ohio, and Washington, D.C., researchers checked his career in those places through reliable primary and secondary sources in Colorado.

It was impossible to ascertain the veracity of several parts of the account, such as Bennet's after-dinner visits with President Lincoln and his interview with Gen. Ulysses S. Grant. Along similar lines, his presence at scenes immediately following the violent physical attacks upon Horace Greeley and Charles Sumner in Washington would have been incredibly difficult to corroborate. Whether or not Bennet helped to stake out Aspen, as he claims, remains unanswered as well. Yet the known facts are such that he easily could have been a participant in or witnessed any one of those events that remain questionable, and in large measure early Colorado historians bear him out.

Furthermore, the memoirs are given in a style that is matter-of-fact, modest, and sometimes wryly humorous. There is little in their delivery that suggests the hand of an imposter or fraud and hardly enough in their drama to entertain for long the speculation that Hiram's novelist son added colorful or fictional details. Bennet's sense of his own role in historic events comes through without fanfare or self-aggrandizement except in those minor—and rather forgivable— moments when he takes pride in recalling that he quieted a crowd of vigilantes or by quick thinking outwitted a pair of highwaymen. Overall, the tone of the memoirs, while not passive, reinforces the role that Bennet played as a witness to historical events rather than as a major actor.

Finally, the authenticity of the document is reinforced by some of its very weaknesses and omissions. The first 166 pages of the transcript, for example, furnish a detailed summary of Bennet's life up to the admission of Colorado as a state, when he was fifty years old, yet his remaining thirty-eight years are condensed all too briefly into 18 pages. Apparently he did not see fit to describe his later life or legal career in any detail, and his silence on this score may indicate that he considered only his early contributions as a pioneer and politician to be of any value for posterity. Similarly, he says very little about his family, his law practice, his friends, or his associates. Surely if this were a work of historical imagination some effort would have been made to construct events, character, and dramatic action into a neater whole. As it is, Bennet, in looking back on his long life, reduces the wealth of his experiences to little more than selected highlights that seem to remain important when all else has fallen away. The recollection of such random but fascinating episodes is not inconsistent with the lapses of old age.

Given these idiosyncrasies, and by using the best available sources together with basic historical methods, the editors believe beyond a reasonable doubt that Bennet's memoirs are authentic and that he represents the early Colorado pioneer and nineteenth-century westerner in many ways.

Hiram Pitt Bennet was born in Carthage, Maine, on September 2, 1826, the fourth of eight sons in the family of Elisha and Maria Bradbury Bennet.[2] In September 1831 the Bennets moved to Galion, Ohio, where Elisha worked as both a toolmaker and a farmer. They moved again in September 1839, this time to northwest Missouri, some twenty-five miles north of St. Joseph.[3] Hiram and his brothers attended what passed for schools in both areas as they cultivated the farm and survived fairly typical boyhoods. After his father's death in 1844, Hiram continued to work on the family farm.

In 1846 the young man decided to become a lawyer and returned to Ohio where he enrolled in private schools for several months before entering Central College in Amalthea in 1847. He then pursued a special course at Ohio Wesleyan until illness and lack of money forced him to withdraw. By then he had gained some schoolteaching experience and, after returning to Missouri, continued to teach in 1850 and 1851 while reading law at night. Upon his admission to the bar in 1851, he moved to Glenwood, Iowa, where he began his practice as a lawyer. The following year he married Sarah McCabe and was elected county judge. Two years later, in 1854, friends persuaded Bennet to move to Nebraska City, Nebraska Territory, where he practiced law and was elected to the first territorial legislature, serving as a member of the upper house.

In 1855 Stephen F. Nuckolls, a prominent merchant and Whig, backed Bennet's candidacy for Congress. The campaign was unsuccessful, and although Bennet journeyed to Washington, D.C., to contest the seat, he still did not win it. The trip was not without some benefit, however, for he learned his way around the capital and in June 1855 attended the Republican convention in Philadelphia, where he was chosen a convention vice-president.

Back in Nebraska, Bennet continued his law partnership until 1857, when he withdrew to serve in the territorial legislature as Speaker of the House. Once more, in 1859, he sought a congressional seat—this time as a Republican who opposed the *spread* of slavery into the territories—but failed to win the nomination of his party. Then, because of intermittent ill health, his brother William's pulmonary consumption, and the effects of the Panic of 1857 on local conditions, he decided to leave Nebraska for the newly discovered Pikes Peak gold fields. The two Bennet brothers sold their Nebraska holdings in the summer of 1859 and, accompanied by their wives, left in September for the Rockies. At their journey's end, they settled in Auraria where Hiram opened a law office.

In some respects, Bennet's background was not unlike that of many easterners who flocked to Colorado during the gold rush. As a child he had twice moved as his family sought its fortunes farther west, and his boyhood had been spent in or near new settlements on the frontier. Yet several things set Bennet apart not only from other Pikes Peakers but also from his fellow westerners in general. These included his formal, if sporadic, education and pursuit of a law degree, his involvement in politics, and his decision to make the journey to the Kansas and Nebraska gold fields in search of physical rather than financial health.

The circumstances of Bennet's arrival in the Pikes Peak region also reflect his intention to stake a claim in the future of this newest of frontiers. Following the popular Platte River route to the gold fields, he left his midwestern home late in the year, and his arrival in the fall of 1859 placed him far behind most of the gold seekers. Yet he was in the vanguard of those providers of goods and services who came later to serve the mining population in the new settlements. Unlike their predecessors, who were out to make a quick fortune and leave, these latecomers brought their wives and families in the hope of becoming permanent inhabitants. Bennet carried law books instead of mining equipment, a sign that he did not plan to hurry to the nearest diggings. He was not a gold seeker but a professional with an abiding interest in politics, bent on establishing himself in a new region.

Very quickly Bennet seized whatever opportunities arose to introduce law, order, and stability into the often unruly twin settlements of Denver and Auraria, which lay on either side of Cherry Creek. With a transient population living far from home and civil war threatening in the East, these dusty little communities faced potentially violent times marked by local events that called for cooler, more experienced heads than many of the residents had. Trained as a jurist, attorney, and politician, Bennet was well equipped to deal with mobs, murders, and mutiny. In less than a year he helped to establish the rule of law over vigilante justice and proved himself capable of preserving the cause of the Union in the Cherry Creek settlements.

One of Bennet's most important accomplishments was the establishment of a regular "People's Court," which may have been inspired by his witnessing two duels and a near-lynching that was prevented only by his successful attempt to sway an angry mob. But he was not alone in these efforts, for Gen. William Larimer, one of Denver's founders, and William N. Byers, editor of the *Rocky Mountain News* and a compatriot of Bennet's in the battle for order, had also sought relief from lawlessness through traditional legal processes. Soon Bennet became a public prosecutor and within thirty days had brought charges against 125 men, whom Judge Jacob Downing promptly sentenced. Bennet also served as judge of an extemporary court, convened after his friend Byers was kidnapped by a group of hoodlums.

Similarly, the activities of southern sympathizers early in the decade kept Unionists like Bennet on constant alert for demonstrations of disloyalty, like the raising of a Confederate flag over the Wallingford and Murphy store. Although in his memoirs he confuses the chronology of events, Bennet countered such expressions with vigor and a good deal of imagination, such as turning Washington's Birthday in 1861 into a celebration of the Union. A man of high public spirit, he turned from that event to head the reception committee and to deliver the welcoming address for the territory's first governor, William Gilpin, on May 27.[4]

Bennet's interest in politics typified men of his generation. This was particularly true in Denver-Auraria, where residents had embroiled themselves in political battles almost from the time the first wagons arrived in September and October of 1858. His enthusiasm and experience paid off, for in the summer of 1861 he defeated Kentuckian and Democrat Beverly D. Williams, delegate of the defunct territory of Jefferson, in a race for the billet of first Colorado territorial delegate to Congress. He was reelected in November 1862 over political rivals J. M. Francisco, who ran strongly in the southern part of the territory, and former governor Gilpin, who was supported by the Abolitionists. Although he could not vote in office, Bennet used his influence to secure a branch mint for Denver as well as postal routes, post offices, a local land office, and military posts for the territory. In the aftermath of the Sand Creek Massacre, he also helped to gain Col. Patrick Conner's appointment as commandant of the Colorado Military District. Later, in 1863, he journeyed to the Far West to purchase ground for a mint in Nevada at the behest of Salmon P. Chase, treasurer of the United States. He ended his busy terms as Colorado's territorial delegate on March 4, 1865, a little more than a month before Lincoln's assassination.

One of the most poignant and fascinating parts of Bennet's memoirs is his description of Abraham Lincoln, with whom he had several conversations in the White House. Although he relates little of great historical substance, Bennet draws a well-rounded portrait of Lincoln and evokes—as he does so well throughout the memoirs—a feeling for the atmosphere of the moment. Similarly, Bennet draws a concise and memorable picture of Gen. Ulysses S. Grant, one of the few other men he admired. In both cases the impact of his observation is the more effective because it is told so sparingly.

Released from his political obligations in 1865, Bennet joined his old friend Stephen F. Nuckolls in New York City where they sold oil lands and Colorado properties for a year before Bennet returned to Denver to practice law.[5] Once again, a political opportunity arose to keep him from full-time commitment to his profession. This time it was his membership on the Indian commission that treated with the Utes between 1866 and 1868 for their lands in western Colorado. He was also among the entourage that accompanied General Grant on his visit to Denver, Central City, and Georgetown in July 1868. Bennet must have impressed the war hero and presidential candidate, for Grant appointed him Denver postmaster in March 1869, a position that Bennet occupied until removed by the president in 1874. His ouster stemmed from the machinations of territorial governor Edward M. McCook, probably the prime example of a carpetbag governor in Colorado Territory. Although the postmaster's position was again tendered to him, Bennet refused it in the prospect of gaining office after Colorado became a state on August 1, 1876. Realizing his goal, Bennet was elected state senator and served during the first session of the state legislature, the last time he was to hold a major political office.

In the fall of 1876 business took Bennet to Deadwood, South Dakota, where, joined by his family, he remained through 1877. In 1878 his son's ill health forced him to return to Denver where he rented a home for his wife and children before heading to Leadville, which was just beginning to boom. True to form, he joined the second wave of hopefuls to enter the flourishing camp. The next year found him working as a right-of-way attorney for the Denver and Rio Grande Railroad. He claims to have helped lay out Aspen before proceeding to Glenwood Springs in 1880.[6] Several years later, in 1885, he obtained an appointment as state agent for federal school lands and worked on other state projects as well. He continued to live in Denver but, even at a time when the city was growing by leaps and bounds and legal fees should have been lucrative, his law practice did not prosper.

The hard times that followed the Panic of 1893, as well as illness, sent Bennet to the rapidly developing East Texas town of Port Arthur in 1897. However, this change of scene proved unhappy: Clara Ames Bennet, his second wife, died there and Bennet's practice did not flourish. By then in his seventies and sickly, he returned to Denver to resume his profession. There, in 1909, he finally received compensation for his services in connection with the school lands, grudgingly granted by a stingy legislature. Yet the success he felt at completing such a drawn-out endeavor was dampened considerably by a fall which left him permanently crippled and forced him to retire. He died on November 11, 1914.

Hiram Pitt Bennet's memoirs not only furnish us with a pioneer's interpretation of Denver's beginnings but also provide an excellent portrait of the early life of a noted Coloradan who grew up on the frontier, understood its culture, and learned how to persuade others to his way of thinking. Like Byers, Evans, and Larimer, Bennet was at the forefront of those who advocated law and order in a contumacious community that lacked a permanent citizenry.[7] Nevertheless, he began to slip from prominence once other city builders started to arrive. His career reached its zenith during his two terms as territorial delegate to Congress in the early to mid 1860s; after that, politicians who were more sophisticated, wealthier, or more capable replaced him. Apparently he formed very few close connections with early Denverites who did succeed, although they thought enough of him to see that he served a term as president of the Society of Colorado Pioneers.[8] In fact, by the 1870s he probably preferred areas such as Deadwood and Leadville, which were in their formative stages, just as Denver had been a decade before. There was work for him in such communities; once their boom periods had passed, there was nothing for him to do.

Similarly, Bennet also ran into financial troubles once Colorado became a state. Reputedly he made money during the 1860s—though it is doubtful that he earned it by practicing law—and his association with Stephen F. Nuckolls indicates that he engaged in mine speculation. Yet, by the middle 1880s his finances had become so straitened that creditors repossessed his home. Much of his income may have been lost in the series of depressions that plagued the United States following 1873, but generally speaking his interest in politics kept him from concentrating on the commercial world, which was so necessary to accumulate wealth during the nineteenth century. While others acquired fortunes, Bennet worked to improve the city of Denver and the new state of Colorado. In particular, his involvement as a state agent to obtain Colorado remuneration for loss of certain school lands proved to be so time consuming that it depleted his bank account and wrecked his law practice. Bennet's fascination with such matters, plus his inability to settle in one place for any length of time, prevented him from holding whatever valuable property he might have earlier possessed, or erecting any large buildings bearing his name, or deriving income from interests in cattle, mining, or railroads as the nineteenth century drew to a close.

Doubtless, clues to Bennet's declining fortunes would have appeared in the memoirs had he devoted more time to describing his later life. Things obviously did not go well for him during those years, and his stature in the community lessened so that in the first decade of the twentieth century, his earlier service to Colorado went almost unrewarded by a later generation's legislature too preoccupied with its own affairs—basically reforms—to concern itself with an aging pioneer. Yet although Bennet's health and prosperity faded, his frontiersman's spirit did not. Indeed, it continued strong enough to let him recount his role as a nineteenth-century westerner even as the West he knew slowly disappeared.

CHAPTER ONE

From Maine to Ohio   1826-1834

ACCORDING to the official and family records, the first ancestor of my name in America was John Bennet, a weaver, son of Peter Bennet of Bristol, England. In 1664 John sailed from Bristol to Jamestown in the colony of Virginia at the age of twenty-three. Being a weaver, he very unlikely had enough money to pay for the voyage. Possibly he came over as a sailor. Or he may have paid his passage by selling his services to one of the Virginia colonists.

Another conjecture is that, like very many Englishmen of the time, he was sold as a bound man by the minions of Charles II. On being restored to the throne, Charles II had given his royal word of honor not to persecute anyone who had sided with Oliver Cromwell and the Protestants against Charles I. But as soon as this second Charles came to power, he began to take revenge against the followers of those who had deposed and executed his father. He ordered the body of Cromwell dug up and hanged. Other Protestants were imprisoned or sent to the colonies as slaves.

There were many "one t" Bennets in England. A Sir John Bennet fought in France against Joan of Arc. And Charles II, after his return to England, made Henry Bennet [the] Earl of Arlington. Our John Bennet, however, was a Puritan and therefore against the monarchists. So, whether or not he had sided openly with the royalists, he may well have been among the thousands of victims sold to the colonies either as outright slaves or as men bound to servitude for a number of years. In any case, though John Bennet came to Virginia in 1664, his presence in the Puritan colony of Massachusetts is not noted until 1670. At that time the records show that he married Deborah Grover. He then moved to Weymouth in "witchcraft time." His last move was to Middleboro, where in March 1687 he bought the old homestead of John Nelson, three miles east of Middleboro and twelve from Plymouth Rock. For

250 years that farm was owned and occupied by a Bennet descended from John.

One of the most notable facts about the family is that for the first five generations, only one husband died as young as 61 years. All other husbands and all wives lived well past 70, three past 80, two past 90, and one wife to 100.

My own branch of the family started with Elisha, younger son of Jacob of the fourth generation. Elisha moved to Chesterville, in the then province of Maine, in 1809. He was an expert toolmaker specializing in the making of steelyards, augers, and all edged tools. His son Elisha, born in Middleboro, 1794, also became expert in the same handicraft. At the age of eighteen, he [the younger Elisha] entered the army of the United States, War of 1812, taking the place of a drafted man, for which he was promised a young cow as bounty. He served until honorably discharged, but he never received the cow. At Chesterville, in 1816, he married my mother, Maria Bradbury, daughter of John Bradbury, who also was of early colonial descent. Long afterwards she received, as his widow, a military land warrant because of my father's participation in the military service of the United States.

I was born in Carthage in what was then Oxford County, now Franklin, State of Maine, on the second of September 1826. It was in a room partitioned off in a long wooden building, the other part of which was used as a blacksmith shop. One of the first, if not the first, sounds that entered my ears must have been the tuneful ring of the anvil.

My first recollection carries me back to Farmington, on the Sand River, a branch of the Androscoggin, when I was three years old. I remember holding a horse at the creek bridge near our house while the rider of the animal went to a spring nearby for a drink. When he returned, he gave me two copper cents, my first money—which made me feel richer than I have ever been since or ever expect to be. That summer and the next winter I attended school at the Nahow schoolhouse, two miles from home. I cried because I had to wear a short petticoat instead of trousers. But I have no recollection of the time when I did not know my letters.

In September 1831, when I was five years old, my father and his brother-in-law, Jonas H. Oakes, emigrated with their families to Galion, Ohio.[9] Besides myself there were my five brothers: Isiah, John, Elisha, Thomas, and Joseph. Father had two horses and a light wagon.

We started from Grandfather Bradbury's farm near Chesterville. Past a post and rail fence, we crossed a little creek and ascended a hill. I was sitting between Mother and Father, who was driving. From the hilltop he pointed off to the right to some blue mountains. "There," he said, "is Carthage, where you were born." The road led off the hill and down the "ridge road" to the ferry on the Androscoggin River, a beautiful stream as clear as crystal. The ferryboat was on the other side; but there was a tin horn tied to a stake near where we stopped. My brother John got out of the wagon and ran to blow the horn. At the call the ferryman brought his boat across and took us and our two wagons over the river.

The next place I remember was the Notch House in the White Mountains. Because of measles in the place, we did not go in for the noon meal but camped for eating out on the common. I also remember the verdant countryside through the Green Mountains and something of the route through the beautiful gorges.

One day, as we journeyed along, my behavior was so naughty that I was set down from the wagon to walk off my ill humor. After a short distance I paused in the road in front of a house. When I stopped, the wagon stopped also, and Mother began coaxing me to come on and get in the wagon. I informed her, with some little firmness, that I would not—didn't have to. Just then a motherly looking woman came out the front doorway of the house and, taking in the situation, called to me to come to her. She said that she wanted a little boy about my size and that I should come in quick before those wagons took me off. I reached our wagon in short order, very well satisfied to be again with my pa and ma.

My next remembrance is of our stopover night at Saratoga Springs, New York. I had a drink of water from Congress Spring. It was also at Saratoga that I ate my first peach and got into Mother's pound cake that same evening and ate enough to last me for the next twenty-four years.

The crossing of the Hudson has passed my memory. At Utica, I think it was, our party boarded a canal boat—teams, wagons, and all—and journeyed by water as far as Lockport. While on that boat I heard much language by the boatmen that was neither Greek nor Latin. At Lockport we passed through the wonderful canal locks and again took to the long western road in our wagons. Somewhere between that town and Erie, Pennsylvania, I recall the folks talking about the roar of Niagara Falls, which they had heard that morning before I wakened.

At this time we were in rather a draggled condition. There had been rains and the roads were muddy and bad. More than once we became the subject of remarks on the part of bystanders. Shortly before reaching Erie, which at that time was a mere village, a young man and his girl came up behind us in a one-horse chaise. As they slowly passed us, they laughed and poked fun at our appearance—to all of which we took no notice. But they had gone not more than a hundred yards ahead, and were still in plain view, when their horse shied at a mud hole, running one wheel up on the bank and the other into the hole. That overturned the chaise enough to spill the bright young couple, fine clothing and all, into the middle of the mud hole. When we came up, Father and my uncle smilingly helped to right matters for them as well as they could. The chagrined couple got in and drove slowly into Erie for repairs.

About the time of this incident, my father pointed out to us several masts sticking up out of the water a short distance offshore in Lake Erie. He thought they were the masts of Perry's fleet, which was scuttled there.[10]

We traveled on in much rain and mud along the lakeshore to the village of Cleveland, Ohio, where we crossed the Cuyahoga River on a float bridge, the only bridge of the kind I had ever seen. Beyond it we plodded south along our weary journey for fifty miles through the beech woods and across points of the Sandusky Plains to Galion, Ohio. There our thousand-mile journey of thirty days ended.[11]

The town was then no more than a few houses—with one store, one tavern, and a sawmill on Whetstone Creek. Old John Ruhl, who lived half a mile out of town to the west on the Bucyrous Road, was the pro-prietary landlord of the town. His son Jake was the tavernkeeper; another son, Mike, the only store[keeper]. Jake also ran the sawmill, one of the old cash-up-and-down kind, when there was enough water in the Whetstone to turn the overshot wheel. He sawed up much cherry and black walnut trees into lumber for common building purposes. At that time, when either of these woods was used for fine furniture, the cabinetmakers veneered the front parts with mahogany.

Our first winter we lived in a vacant cabin on a farm three miles from Galion. Much of the time we were scarce of bread owing to winter floods in the millstreams which prevented the mills from grinding. We had an abundance of frostbitten potatoes and salt meat. Father was sick most of the cold weather and could do nothing towards support-ing his family.

When the millstones started grinding, we got a grist of flour, and Mother made a shortcake, quite a large one. She baked it on a poplar board set up on edge, with a flatiron behind to hold it as near as possible before the fire. We of course had no stove. All cooking was done in a fireplace. It was the sweetest bread I ever tasted.

That winter my next older brother, Elisha, and myself had fun doing what children nowadays might not consider amusing. We would take off our footwear and make dashes out into the snow, which was from two to six inches deep, to see who could run the farthest out and get back without freezing his feet.

In the spring of 1832 Father sold his team and moved us into Galion. There he built a house of black walnut and poplar lumber on the main street opposite Bentley's tavern. He also opened a blacksmith shop, and, though still not very well, was able to work a good part of the time. He was a very ingenuous [ingenious] smith, the best in all that region. He could make anything out of iron or steel that was called for—steelyards, augers, broadaxes, chopping axes, drawing knives for shaving shingles, and knives of all kinds. All edged tools he tempered just hard enough to take the sharpest edge and not so soft as to bend or break. The Collins chopping ax was of factory make, brought from the East and sold to woodchoppers. The steel in them was good, but for some reason it did not hold a good, sharp edge. Many of the Collins [axes], when taken from the country store, would be brought to Father's shop for him to "up-set" the blades, as it was called, and temper them before they were used. Many other axes he made outright from Sweded bar iron for the pole and cast steel for the blade. The Collins axes were of uniform weight. Father would make an ax of any weight or shape the customer might want. He had bought his anvil but made his own bellows.

My oldest brother, Isiah, was old enough to help Father in the shop. He would blow the bellows and then swing with both hands the heavy sledge on the hot iron, which Father held on the anvil with tongs in his left hand while giving alternate blows with the hand-hammer in his right. Work came into the shop faster than Father could turn it out. There was so much horseshoeing to be done that he was not strong enough to do it all. But because of the good profit in that work, after a few months he built another forge and took on William Johnson, a stout young fellow from Wooster, Ohio, as a "jour" or journeyman. He shod all the horses that came. Father also built a frame shed outside the shop to shoe oxen, which he himself shod.

The streets of Galion were very muddy in springtime. It was the fashion with boys and even the men to cross them on stilts, as the mud was over ankle deep.

The following August, Enos Johnson and Pete Traub, boys about my own age, and myself discovered a wild cherry tree loaded with ripe fruit. We climbed it and ate our fill. Enos's father was a doctor, and Enos managed to get home. I didn't. Searchers found me in a patch of elderberry bushes, very sick and unconscious. Pete was found in about the same condition. About three o'clock the next morning I returned to consciousness. Father was holding me in his arms, and the doctor, who was standing over me, said that I was better. I became unconscious again but at last recovered. It was a severe but good lesson for little boys who knew no better than to fill up their stomachs with wild cherries, pits and all.

There were many swamps in the country around Galion full of frogs, and the trees and bushes surrounding the same were great resorts of blackbirds, singing and nesting. The woods also had many squirrels, racoons, and possums. There were a few deer and more wolves; no elk, but now and then a bear or a panther.

For a few years after our arrival in Ohio, the sun in the spring was occasionally darkened for an hour or so in the afternoon by immense flocks of passenger pigeons. They numbered millions as they flew over our town to their roosting grounds in the dense woods on the Maumee. All these birds and animals found in the woods an abundance of food in the way of beechnuts, chestnuts, hickory nuts, black walnuts, acorns, and many other kinds of nuts besides mulberries, black and red raspberries, wild grapes, black haws, ginseng, and other wild foods. The wild animals and birds did not consume all this mast; there was too much of it. Enough was left for the "woods hogs" to fatten on in the fall and for we boys to gather and store for cracking on winter nights.

There were six boys of us in the family when we came to Ohio, all under fourteen. From the beginning of 1833 to the end of 1836 we flourished in poverty but were never entirely destitute. With the help of us boys and Mother's ceaseless toil, Father was able to provide our family with scant clothing and enough food to grow on. The cloth came from Mother's spinning wheel and hand loom.

Poor as were nearly all of our fellow pioneers, most were usually ready to help less fortunate neighbors. One time when we took some meal to the cabin of a widow, her boy called from the doorway: "What you got? Maw says we done taking in barley." Our parents managed to keep the younger of us in such schools as there were then. I attended three months in summer and two in winter until I was nine years old.

Learning in those days was imparted in a manner somewhat different than at present. It was not particularly enjoyable to hold out my small hands, tough as they were, for the palms to be whacked with a beech ruler. Nor did any of us little fellows enjoy sitting on the hard benches, which were so high that our feet could not touch the floor. It was forbidden for us to swing our legs; but when they ached they would not stay still. As a consequence, many little shins were bruised by that same beech ruler. We had no screaming, romping games in the open air to break the dreary routine of study and recitation. School was every weekday. It took up at seven in the morning and let out at five, with an hour's recess at noontime.

U. S. mails were carried on horseback, once a week. The postage on one-sheet letters was twenty-five cents, double that for two sheets. Letters were folded and sealed with a wafer. No envelopes.

In the spring of 1833, as I remember, I was wakened by Father about two o'clock one morning and told to come out and see the wonderful sight of the stars falling. Sure enough, I saw the sky sparkling with falling meteors—to us real stars—shooting across and down in every part of the heavens. It was too cold for me to stay very long, so I ran back to my trundle bed. The "stars" did not stop falling until after daylight—not indeed until eleven o'clock on that day.

In the morning, Johnathan Fellows, our Methodist neighbor, came over to the smith shop to discuss the great event with Father, who was regarded as a pretty smart, learned man, being a Yankee. With a most solemn air, Johnathan asked Father if he did not think that these were "the last days when the stars should fall from heaven." Father answered: No, that when he was out looking at the falling stars, he had taken a few sniffs of the air and had not smelled any brimstone, so he did not think the end of the world had yet come. Brother Fellows looked very solemn, and as he was passing out of the door, he said there would be a prayer meeting that evening at the schoolhouse.

My father did not believe in a personal devil, nor in a literal hell of fire and brimstone in the future world. He was called a Universalist because he believed that God was the Father of mankind and would take care of His children without resorting to a miracle to keep them alive hereafter in order to torture them forever in burning brimstone. It can be imagined what hot discussions he had with the ignorant fanatics and bigoted preachers in the neighborhood. He could quote and apply more of the Scriptures than any of them in these arguments.

During 1834 a Colonel Newman came out from Maine to Ohio. He was called "colonel" because he had a few hundred dollars more than anybody in our neighborhood. As Father's emigrant fever was still unabated, he induced the colonel to join him in a trip west to Illinois to look at the country. They went off together on two of Newman's horses, and were away about two months.

Father was well pleased with the Fox country. He wanted the colonel to invest in some land in such a way that Father could bring out his family and settle on a place. As they rode over the beautiful prairie, the colonel virtually agreed to this and to bring out his own family as well.

But it happened that some western men were stopping at the tavern that night, and the colonel heard them talking together. They were praising the country, expressing great faith in its future, etc., talking to themselves, not to the colonel or Father.

The colonel broke in on the party in a very pompous manner. He loudly asserted that the country would never amount to a continental unless it was settled and developed by men of money and enterprise from New England. The men ceased talk while the colonel was addressing them, then went on with their conversation, ignoring the colonel's speech without a word or further look towards him. The colonel was very much disgusted by this disregard of him. He withdrew from the room and informed my father that they would start home the next morning. That was the end of Father's hopes to get a home in Illinois. He and the colonel returned to Galion, and a few days later the colonel hitched up his teams and went back to Maine, where the common people had more respect for his great wisdom and wealth.

CHAPTER TWO

Frontier Boyhood   1835-1838

IN 1835, as I remember, the Potawatomies, Shawnees, and Wyandots were removed to the West. The Potawatomies settled in western Iowa, the others in Kansas—then known as the Kaw River country. By this we lost all of our roving but peaceable red neighbors who had been living thirty or forty miles from us in the Sandusky Plains. In 1836 Father bought from Oreal Straw for $400 a farm or "clearing," as it was called, about three miles from Galion. On it was a log barn and a log house with an open fireplace and brick oven. He sold his house and shop in town, but built and used a smith shop on the farm while we boys worked the land. About thirty acres were in cultivation; the rest was still primeval forest of white and red oak, beech, sugar maple, poplar, cherry, chestnuts, and elms.

In most localities at that time, trees were a nuisance to the settler. Before he could so much as plant a crop, he had to clear his ground, acre by acre, by chopping and burning up the trees. Until 1839 the main part of my education consisted of learning to swing an ax in the woods and clearing the land of trees and brush; also to hog corn, harvest the crops, and make sugar and syrup from the sap of the sugar maples.

For two or three months each, during the last four years, I attended a subscription school a mile or so away. The place, a one-room log cabin with a big open fireplace, was called the Rogers schoolhouse because it stood on land belonging to a man of that name. One winter I lived with Rogers and did chores for my board. He, however, had no more to do with the running of the school than did the rest of the neighbors. As was common at that time in those parts, a would-be teacher, or someone who wished his children to attend school, would pass around a paper on which parents signed up to pay so much per pupil. The children of those who subscribed made up the school.

Our spelling book was Websters, succeeded by the Elementary. When I got as far as the pictures in the back part of Websters, I then was given the English Reader, and read in the first class, standing with others in line "toeing the mark"—a crack in the floor. In 1838 the teacher was James Dunlap, a man of sandy complexion. He knew something of arithmetic, nothing of grammar, wrote a fairly good copy, and could make a good pen. We used goose quills for pens in those days. He was a teacher who encouraged learning in his pupils, especially spelling.

I was one of the best spellers in his school; none better except my oldest brother Isiah. That winter we had "spelling schools" (contests) galore, at least one night a week. Choosing the best spellers first, our captains divided the school into opposite sides. The words were given out by the teacher, beginning at the head of the column, and if misspelled, then to his opponent, alternating from side to side until the word was spelled right. A count was kept to show which side missed the most. The crucial test was at the last when, if one missed a word, he sat down. This would soon reduce the number standing to a few of the best spellers. The excitement would become more and more intense as the contest continued, until all on one side or the other were spelled down. Schools of different districts frequently met in these matches and contested for victory. Sometimes the teachers of their schools would join in and spell with their pupils.

The 1838 school term closed in March, when all pupils had to start their spring farming. But James Dunlap did not lose thought of his two months school, the only one he ever taught, nor of the very talented pupils whom he had discovered. So, in May of that year, at no little expense to himself, he fitted up the threshing floor of his big new barn and organized a theatrical exhibition among his late pupils. To this all people around that region were invited, seats free. Hundreds came. The day was bright and warm, perfect picnic weather, and most everyone brought a lunch. The orchestra consisted of one bass drum, a kettle or snare drum, a fife, and two fiddles. After the audience was all seated and the band had executed some patriotic airs, including 'The Girl I Left Behind Me," the curtain was drawn, and the exhibition began with the dialogue between Brutus and Cassius, from Shakespeare. Next was an oration on eloquence from the Columbian Orator, followed by more music from the orchestra.

Then came the tragedy of David and Goliath. This was my first and only appearance before the footlights. Though only twelve years old and small for my age, I had been chosen to act as David. Abner Sharrock was Goliath, and looked it. He stood six feet two in his socks and weighed two hundred pounds. For a helmet, the great Goliath had donned an immense empty hornets' nest, which made him eight feet high. His spear was a hickory handspike the same height. His armor was a buckeye "wammus," homespun trousers that badly bagged at the knees, and heavy cowhide boots. As David, I was clad in homespun wammus and trousers, hatless and barefoot, and armed only with a sling.

Goliath walked up and down the stage (the barn floor) bullying and defying the army of the Israelites. David came in and said he was ready to fight him so he might as well cease his "bloviating." This challenge from the diminutive David, without armor or arms except a shepherd's sling, disgusted Goliath. He scorned to fight, but David insisted. With much braggadocio, Goliath taunted how he would impale the little fellow on his spear. When Goliath said he trusted in his great spear, David rejoined: "I trust in Heaven. The God of Battles stimulates my arm and fires my soul with ardor not its own."

When Goliath came at me from the farther side of the floor, I, David, swung my sling and let fly a potato ball. The hurled missile struck the giant in the center of his forehead, and the great fellow fell heavily to the floor. I ran to him, and drawing out his sword—a long corncutter blade—cut off his "head" and swung up the hornets' nest before the audience, amid great applause. Then I recited "The September Gale" by Oliver Wendell Holmes, which had recently been published in our county paper. I came out without any change of costume and declaimed the piece with great *eclat*—to judge by the applause. This, my first and last appearance on the boards as an actor, fully established at the time my reputation as a star of the first magnitude in all the country round about. And yet I did not begin to hook watermelons for a year or more afterwards.

On the third of July that year, Father told [us] that if we boys finished up first plowing and hoeing of the cornfield, we might have the next day for a holiday in town. There great preparations were in process for celebrating the Fourth with such foolish things as making big noises with gun, anvil or cannon, and with soldiers parading. We made the work fly, and by eight the next morning were able to come into breakfast and tell Father the job was finished on time. After breakfast, of which I ate but little, being so anxious to get to town, he gave my two oldest brothers, Isiah and John, seventy-five cents each in Mexican quarters, and to my next older brother, Elisha, and myself twenty-five cents each—all to spend in town that day as we pleased. We lost little time over our scant breakfast and hurried over the three miles to town barefoot, feeling with all our money like country gentlemen.

Before we had gone far, we heard the firing of the anvils and later the base drum. Then came the music of the fifes and the faraway sight of the flag and the glistening bayonets of the marching soldiers. It was a most glorious Fourth. The militia was out for training, with such fine caps and feathers. Oh, but it was a time! The music was so exhilarating to me and there was such a lot of people that I did not think of anything to eat until along in the afternoon. At last my eldest brother got sight of me and gave me a big piece of his gingerbread. It tasted very good, but while eating it I did not fail to keep up with the music and marching.

Night fell before the celebration came to an end. Then we boys got together with other boys of our neighborhood and started for home through the beech woods. A lot of tired limbs and bare feet got into bed that night. The next morning I could hardly get around before eight or nine o'clock to join my brothers in the commencement of the second plowing and hoeing of the corn. But we all enjoyed talking over that good time for weeks afterwards.

In our farm spring-house the spring was enclosed in a section of a large, hollow sycamore log. We could dip out the water from the top of the curb. The overflow formed a "spring run" that flowed through the lower room of the spring-house over a flagstone trench. In this Mother set the milk and butter crocks, keeping their contents cool in the hottest weather.

That fall we did some post-and-rail fencing along the roadside. The ground was soft and sloppy, and Jake Crow had not yet come along to make up our winter shoes. Much of the time we all suffered from cold feet. During the winter I was kept out of school by sickness, perhaps as a result of that exposure.

Circumstances make quite a difference as to the enjoyableness of being sick. At the age of six I had had scarlet fever and had found it a serious trial, for there were lots of boys around with whom I liked to play. But when, six years later, the measles took me at harvest time I was not altogether sorry to be sick. It was then, in 1837, that I was first inspired with ambition to become a great man. Of all seasons of the year, harvest time on a farm is the best time for a barefoot boy to have measles. Sharp stubble cut the feet, and carrying together two heavy sheaves of grain is not pleasant to a young boy.

Well, when I began to get better from my sickness, being yet too weak to get out of bed, I wanted something to entertain or amuse me.

Mother got down for me Weems's *Life of Washington.* I had never before read the book but had often heard what a great, good man Washington was. Though suffering with dizziness and headache, I read the book through with eagerness. To encourage me, Mother from time to time would dwell upon the great deeds of "the father of our country" and the fact of his being good and truthful when a boy—talk just like mothers make to their own boys—or should. This caused me to think I could in a few years become as great or even a bigger man than Washington—if we could have another war with the British.

Oh, what big brave things I resolved to do while tumbling on my bed and reading that book. Though all too soon, I got well and strong enough to help stack the wheat and oats, [yet] I held to my childish ambition to become a great man.

Grain was reaped with cradle-scythes, to swing which, according to jokers, a man required a strong back and a weak head. Neighbors would join together in a harvest gang, starting in first on the ripest grain and working through field to field until the last had been harvested. My work was to bring water and whiskey to the merry reapers, and, as I have told, to gather together the sheaves for shocking. When the harvesting at each farm was all done, a milk pan full of eggnog was served to the crowd. More or less of maple sugar (we had no cane suger) would remain in the pan after the liquid contents had been drained off by the men. When I removed the pan it is easy to guess I did not forget the sugar.

CHAPTER THREE

Ohio to Missouri   1839

IN THE SUMMER of 1839, Father sold our farm and built two wagons in which to emigrate on west. He made every part of them—wheels, iron tires, and gear. The boxes were each twelve feet long and made of walnut. The running gear was of oak. Handsomely painted, they were the finest looking wagons in that section of the country. The latter part of September we made our start. Abram Hays accompanied us as one of the family, and also old Tom Smith and his family. The intention was to settle in the Osage country, Missouri, near the Ozark Mountains. The roads through Ohio were not bad, our teams were good, and the wagon loads light. We traveled in the usual frontier style, camping out and sleeping in the wagons.

Among the first towns through which we passed were Delaware and Worthington. At the latter place we met my uncle Benjamin Bradbury of Chesterville, Maine. He was teaching music, and Father said he taught the right kind—the round notes. We boys had known only the "buckwheat" notes.[12] Uncle Ben was a fine violinist. He could enthuse an audience and bring them to their feet singing such songs as "Ship A-hoy!"

Beyond Worthington we continued our journey through Columbus and Dayton, Ohio, to Richmond, Indiana. There we rested for a day and took time to look around the town. One of my elder brothers bought *Alonzo and Melisee.* I bought *The Children of the Abbey* in four pretty little volumes. I felt very grown-up, it being my first purchase. But I had no opportunity to read it until the following winter, after our journey's end, and then only by firelight. That meant lounging on the hearth, with my head close to the flickering blaze that scorched the top of my coarse sealskin cap and nearly baked my brains, so eager was I to read the silly novel.

Resuming our journey along the National Turnpike, we passed through Indianapolis, at that time not much larger than Galion. Then came Terra Haute, the last town in Indiana, where we crossed the Wabash on a bridge. Next was the old French town of Vandalia, then the capital of the state of Illinois. From there we plodded westerly through a prairie country. At Edwardsville we lost the company of Tom Smith and his family. Old Tom had not told us he was going to "back out." But in the morning we were ready to start first, and he said for us to go on ahead; that he would catch up. That was the last we saw of him or his family. We boys thought it was all due to the fact that our dog could "lick" and outrun his dog. But I afterwards concluded that the feebleness of his wife and the length of the journey that lay before us were the reasons which induced him to turn aside and settle in Illinois.

We passed by many fine orchards and farms between Vandalia and Alton, on the Mississippi River. It was perhaps a better country for us in which to settle than the one we were bound for. But Father did not think so. At Alton we crossed the Mississippi, which Father said was the largest river in the United States. We had camped on the near bank at nightfall. In the morning we crossed over by ferry, a boat worked with oars by two stout men. The weather was foggy, but we got safely over. Then was when I saw my first steamboat.

We passed across the Mississippi bottomlands through large cotton-wood timber. On our way along the north side of the Missouri River, a few miles below Alton, we saw many large orchards. They had been planted by the French sixty or seventy years before, and at this time were apparently abandoned. We did not lack for apples on the way. After passing St. Charles, a man riding a good horse and dressed in homemade Kentucky jeans and a big broad-brimmed brown hat over-took us and rode along beside our wagon for some little time, talking with Father. After satisfying himself who we were, he explained that, owing to our fine wagons, he had taken us for Mormons going to Indianapolis but was glad to find that we were not. He said he lived in the country we were passing through; that he had been in the Osage country to which we were going, and also up in the Platte Purchase. The latter, which was on our side of the river, he said consisted of some five or six counties of fine timber and prairie land. It was much better for new settlers than the Osage country, where there was much fever and ague.

A year before, the Purchase had been made by treaty with the Indians, who then moved farther west, across the river, opposite St. Joseph. Still more of the friendly advice that he gave us resulted in our changing our objective point from the Osage country to the Platte Purchase. We crossed the Chariton River, a northerly branch of the Missouri, and camped on the farther bank. That evening I helped eat a six-pound buffalo fish. The man who brought it to us sat by the campfire and talked with us for some time. He was quite a fellow, with little education but of a friendly disposition, though he hated Mormons. He knew a great deal about the country we were now in.

Among other things, he told us about the fights which had resulted in driving away the Mormons from Independence, Missouri, to Nauvoo, Illinois. According to his account, there had been considerable shooting. One of his acquaintances, he said, "was shot right through the head, and right smart of his brains ran out; but he got over it." Father smiled, and the next day he remarked to us that the man was a great storyteller, for nobody could possibly live after their brains had been disturbed by a bullet. Since then I have learned that Father was mistaken.

Our road now lay across Wahcandough Prairie, which was thickly covered with dry grass four or five feet high. From the middle of the prairie there were not any settlements in sight. One of us boys thought he would like to see a prairie fire. He started a little blaze by the roadside. The wind sprang up and in a minute the fire spread and raged fearfully. It swept forward and to our left. Farther on we saw too late what a dangerous thing we had done. Off to the left, a mile or more away, were settlements directly in the line of the fire. There were women and children on the sheds and houses looking at the approaching danger. We hurried on across the prairie as fast as we could and camped that night at Richmond, in Hay County. After seeing the spread of the fire that we had so innocently started, we were in no little fear and expected the sheriff would be following us with a warrant for our arrest. We did not feel free from apprehension until we reached Liberty in Clay County. There we bought the last barrel of flour we were to have until we raised wheat on our own farm for milling.

Driving on from Liberty, we crossed the Little Platte River at Agency Ford and passed along the Blacksnake Hills into Buchanan County. The Sac and Fox tribes had only recently vacated their village near this place to move on westward across the river. Their scalp tree, or pole, and much vermilion paint were to be seen about the abandoned village. There were also many of their graves around. Six miles below the Indian post, we found shelter in two cabins belonging to Bob

Duncan; one, ten by twelve, being occupied by ourselves, and the other by our livestock. Next morning, November 23, we wakened up in a tremendous snowstorm. For the next three weeks we had to remain there stormbound. During that time a sled was made, and Father and two of the older boys went up into Andrew County exploring for a place to settle. When they returned, I had been laid up by a kick on the knee from a horse.

They had found a place, and we broke camp at once. After the wagons started on, Mother and the small children and myself were put on the sled to follow. We stopped at Robidoux's trading post, where we saw several Frenchmen and trappers and a number of Indians.[13] Father went into the store to buy something, but I lay helpless on the sled on account of my knee.

Besides trading with the Indians, Robidoux dealt in goods and supplies for the incoming white settlers. Stacked up in his place, he had bale upon bale of buffalo robes and the skins of bears, beaver, and other animals. To round out the rich odors of the premises, a few Indians lounged about. Had I been blind and deaf, my nose would have been able to tell me that we were in Indian country.

The post was then on the very outskirt of civilization, in fact beyond the border other than for the few rude appliances of civilization that we immigrants brought with us from the beech woods of Ohio. Old Joe Robidoux had spent most of his life trading among the Indians, by whom he was greatly liked. It was otherwise, however, with his Negroes, when, two years later, he laid out his land for the town of St. Joseph in honor of his patron saint. It was said that, in his town building, he hired from their owners a great many black slaves and that he was a hard taskmaster, working his laborers early and late and feeding them but poorly. I used to hear the Negroes sing of the fare he gave them:

A little cold coffee and the meat very fat,
and Robidoux he grumble if you eat much of dat.
    Up jamboree! who, who!
    Up jamboree! who! who!

On the whole, notwithstanding, Robidoux was a very good man, in his way, on the western frontier.

That night we stopped with Sam Davis, a man whom we had known in Ohio. The next day we moved into a log cabin near Davis's place. It was about twenty feet square, had a puncheon floor and a large open fireplace. Overhead, reached by ladder, was a loft where we boys slept. Here we went into winter quarters, nine of us all told, and lived on corn bread and salt pork until spring.

During the January thaw, we boys had lots of fun hunting coons and bees. On warm nights the coons would leave their tree holes and go visiting to neighbor coons in other hollow trees. In the morning we would track them in the snow and catch them by felling the trees in which they had their holes. Our dog did the killing. We also found several bee trees from the way the bees cleaned house on the warmest of the winter days, throwing out their refuse on the clean snow. To get the honey, we would cut down the bee tree on a cold day and rob the hive without danger of getting stung. There were plenty of deer and wild turkeys about, but we lacked both guns and skill for such game. Though we never relished coon or possum, we had all the prairie chicken and squirrels we wanted.

In the spring, under the Preemption Acts of 1840 and 1841, Father entered three quarter-sections of rich prairie land about four miles north of the present town of Savannah, the county seat of Andrew County.[14] On this claim we built the first house on the prairie in that region, a double-hewed log cabin. After we fenced our land, the county road ran alongside of it with the fence of Terhune's land across from us. The road was named Bennet's Lane and became famed as the muddiest piece of road in northwest Missouri.

CHAPTER FOUR

Indian Country 1840-1846

FROM THAT SPRING of 1840 to 1846, I worked on the farm with my brothers the year round. It was work, work, work, and no school, no play, and nothing to read except the Bible, hymn books and occasional copies of the *Louisville Journal* and *St. Louis Republican.*

We raised crops of corn, wheat, oats, flax, hemp and potatoes. No rye, barley, or millet but [a] great abundance of pumpkins and squash. The first plowing was of the primitive sod, called "breaking the prairie," done with the prairie plow drawn by four or five yoke of oxen. The second year furrowing was with an ordinary two-horse plow, about six inches deep. The saying was: "Plow deep while sluggards sleep, and you'll have corn to sell and keep." After plowing, the ground was harrowed to break up the lumps, then laid out in rows both ways, four feet apart, and the corn planted in hills. Small grain was sown broadcast by hand and covered by the harrow.

Of all that we raised on the farm, we could sell for cash nothing except hemp. This was easy to plant and grow. But cutting, retting, and breaking was hard, dusty work. Delivered at the river landing, six miles away, it brought only $2.50 per bale of 112 pounds. Corn could be bought for ten cents a bushel; fifty cents a "barl"—five bushels. Prices for horses and cattle were very low with no ready sale, and no cash market at that.

J. N. Prather, the richest man in all the county, was said to be worth $20,000. Everybody else was too poor to buy store goods. However, we made out fairly well with plain homemade clothing, cut from cloth spun and woven by Mother from our own flax and wool. Like ourselves, most families had their own looms and spinning wheels. The first year or two we had little more to eat than "hog and hominy," except in the fall for the luscious wild blackberries.

Before stoves came along, we cooked before an open fire of hickory, maple, or beech wood. In Ohio we had baked bread and beans in a brick oven, built in the wall alongside the fireplace. In Missouri we had bake kettles and skillets with large covers, all cast iron, thick and heavy. The heat would be kept up by hot coals under the skillet and on the cover. There was an iron crane, with hooks, attached to the side of the fireplace. On this, pots could be swung over the fire to cook meat and vegetables for a "boiled" dinner. We also had a tin oven, called a reflector, which was set before the fire. Its low wall sloped down and its upper one up the bread in a pan midway between. The lower surface reflected the heat under and baked the lower crust; the upper surface reflected the heat down and baked the upper crust.

Before leaving Ohio, the Hardings had given me some cloth for helping them with their fall crop. [In] the winter of 1839-40, from this cloth, Mother made me up a pair of trousers and a wammus. The latter was a sleeved sack, loose, short and wide, and was tied in front by the corners in a hard knot. Being tight around the waist, the garment afforded plenty of pocket room next to the body for apples, peaches, etc., not to mention the walnuts, hickory nuts, and chestnuts with which the autumn woods of Ohio so abounded. In Missouri, however, there was little chance for me to use my wammus for such purposes. Nonetheless, I found it of service, seeing that it was the only jacket or coat that I possessed.

From the first, my cloth trousers were patched on the knees and seat with buckskin, also with bands of the same material about the bottom of the legs. I wore these trousers until they bagged so at the knees that nobody thought I had straight legs. They lasted a year or more of steady wear. They were succeeded by trousers of tow cloth, also reinforced with buckskin.

The next winter I had to have a pair of new shoes. I had gone barefoot all summer and fall. There were no shoemakers in the country. Father could find nothing to fit my feet at old Bob Elliot's store on Hackberry Ridge except a pair of stub-toed boots. When I tried on those boots they were about a sixteenth of an inch too short. But I had to have something, and as they were the first boots I had ever had, I told Father they fitted me just right. He said they were too short, but finally let me have them. Though they crippled my feet, I had the proud satisfaction of being the possessor of boots and buckskin trousers—which none of the other boys had.

In the spring of 1840 our cows strayed off. I rode around the country many miles for two weeks before finding them. During my search I sometimes saw as many as sixty or seventy deer feeding on the prairie. When alarmed, they would run off into the hazel brush. There were also plenty of coyotes about and some of the large buffalo wolves.

To go back to the winter of 1839-40, we bought smoked bacon of a Mr. Netes on Lincoln Creek for $2.50 a hundred pounds. Our first crop of corn was ground at Lincoln's mill on the same creek. This Lincoln was said to be a cousin of Abraham Lincoln. Like the latter, he was large and bony and in other respects favored him enough to be a relative. We took our corn in long bags, horseback, and waited our turn to have it ground, as the miller, Lincoln, first took out toll of one eighth a bushel, using a toll-dish for that purpose. According to the rhyme: "The miller quite boldish dived in with his toll-dish and helped himself well for his labor. But the farmer with plenty measured out scanty when he sold any corn to his neighbor."

There lived near us a lot of Tennesseans, good neighbors but very illiterate. Their conversation was much qualified by the Negro accent, tone, and manner of expression. This kind of talk sounded very funny to us when we first came to know them. Tommy Holland, a brave, bold fellow, delighted to entertain us in this peculiar southern dialect with accounts of his experiences under Andrew Jackson in the Creek War. He made frequent use of the word "going," pronouncing it "gwine." Sassy boy that I was, I nicknamed him "old Mr. Gwine." When he heard that I had so called him he was mad, and after that I kept out of his reach.

On Christmas Eve, 1840, we went the rounds of the neighborhood, shouting and making a great noise. At all the neighbors' houses, wherever we called, we were kindly entertained with twister-cakes and in some places with drink stronger than water. This celebrating we kept up until morning. It was, however, only the beginning of our Christmas fun. After breakfast we met together again and went up to the north prairie with a pair of race horses and some dogs. Though most of us were afoot, we expected to catch all wolves in the county before night. A slight skiff of soft snow had fallen and frozen. That left the ground hard and smooth. We raced over the prairie all day until dark without catching a single wolf. Tired and sorry, we separated and returned to our homes.

Christmastime in Missouri was a free week for the slaves. There were several plantations or farms in our locality worked by slave labor. The darkies would put in the daytime of their holidays breaking hemp to earn money with which to frolic and dance during the night. I had learned to break hemp but never earned much money that way. It was very hard labor, using a heavy wooden frame like a flam-break but much larger. Yet I managed to break one whole crop by myself one year.

One winter my brother John taught school, and Elisha did the same the next winter. I attended neither school, as Isiah needed my help with the work at home. But I went to the spelling contests, which, as in Ohio, we held at the schoolhouse once a week. There I maintained a high reputation as a good speller. On such important occasions, I wore a yellow bandana handkerchief around my neck. This, with my boots and buckskins, made me, I thought, a very captivating fellow at the age of fifteen, and a favorite with the girls—maybe.

At sixteen I was tall and wiry and rated as one of the grown men of the family. The "children," my younger brothers, were Joseph, born in 1831, and William, born in 1836. A baby, David, was born and died in 1842. In the fall of that year, the mill stream failed of enough water to run the gristmills. We were hard put to it for bread. At first the only resort was to grate corn on the cob. We plucked the ears just as the grain was out of the silk and beginning to harden. Father made a tin grater about fifteen inches long and fastened it to a board. With the lower end in a pan, the upper against the chair between our legs, and an ear of corn in both hands, we raked up and down on the grater. The result was a moist corn meal that I thought made the very best of bread.

The corn soon became hard as it ripened on the stalk. Father then made a hand mill. It consisted of an upper stone on a pivot to turn around on a stationary lower stone, both stones about fifteen inches in diameter. There was a three-inch hole through the center of the upper one to feed the mill, and a small wooden handle set in a socket on its edge. This mill was run by the muscle power of my brothers and myself with much sweating. We would seize the handle with one hand and twist the upper stone around as fast as we could while with the other hand feeding the corn, a few grains at a time, through the center hole. It took an hour's work, very tiresome on the arms, to grind enough meal for a breakfast. For two months that fall we got our bread by the grating and hand-mill processes.

In the spring of 1843 Isiah married Clarissa Ashley. I think she may have been a granddaughter of General Ashley, who made a fortune in the fur trade two decades before and in the thirties was lieutenant governor of Missouri and later on Missouri's representative in Congress. Her father was a Captain Ashley. Major Miller, then Indian agent for the Pawnees and other tribes west of the Missouri, stopped a few days in our neighborhood on his way to the agency. He offered Isiah the position of blacksmith and gunsmith for the Indians. So Isiah took his young wife and joined Mr. Tabor, a missionary, Mr. Alice, a teacher, and other government employees. All went in wagons to the Pawnee village on Willow Creek, a tributary of Loup Fork, not a great distance from where is now the town of Columbus, Nebraska.

All west of the Missouri was then Indian country and full of Indians. There were Pawnees, Poncas (Comanches), Omahas and Otoes, Sacs and Foxes, Wyandots, and others—all up and down the west bank of the river for three hundred miles. On the near side the Potawatomis occupied what are now the [Iowa] counties of Fremont, Mills, and Pottawattamie. Their tribe extended from the Missouri River many miles east into the then territory of Iowa, including the waters of the Nishinebodony [Nishnabotna] and the headwaters of the Tarkio and Nodaway, which flowed southwest through the northwest part of Missouri into the Missouri River. One or two day's travel took the party with which my brother was a member into and across the territory occupied by the Potawatomi tribe. Crossing the Missouri they drove up the north side of the Platte River ninety miles west to the Pawnee mission.

At that time the Pawnees formed a very large and vigorous tribe. Their chiefs and warriors were tall and of splendid physique. This was particularly true of Falki, their great war chief, head of all the different bands of the tribe. He was over six feet tall, of perfect form, and in every look and action showed plainly that he was born to command. Falki and my brother Isiah became great friends. This was in great part due to the fact that Isiah was so skillful and so accommodating in repairing the firearms of Falki and his braves. Guns were then just being introduced among the Pawnees, who had been armed only with bows and arrows, lances and tomahawks. My brother was also very expert in making pipe-tomahawks of steel. They were in great demand among the Indians, who were very proud of them.

Major Miller's Bellevue Agency in Nebraska was near Sarpy's trading post on the west bank of the Missouri River. During the fall of 1843 the major engaged Father to supply the agency with flour. In October I was given charge of the delivery of the flour, which was hauled by our own ox team and the teams of our neighbors. Two new government employees, a farmer and a blacksmith, accompanied me.

After reaching the Potawatomi country, we took what was then called the ridge road, or trail, instead of the road along the Missouri River bottom. Our road ran along the summit of the divide between the big river and the Nishnabotna. It was high, rolling prairie all the way until we crossed Mosquito Creek, where we turned down west to reach the Missouri.

When out on this road, it was remarked that the country never could be settled because of the lack of timber. The neighbors who were with me thought that it would always remain Indian country and afford a fine market for our horses, breadstuffs, and other supplies.

Crossing over the Missouri in a Mackinaw boat, we delivered the flour to the Bellevue Agency. To return homeward we took the bottom road. This was partly beaten until we passed the farms of some Indians and half-breeds, beyond which there were only Indian trails. The trip down through the bottom through the tall dry grass was hurriedly made. We were afraid of prairie fires, which would have put us in great danger. We were much relieved when we reached the eastern bluffs, where was located the Potawatomi Agency in [the] charge of Major Cooper.

When we came to the agency, we stopped an hour or two to rest and bait our horses and oxen. But on approaching the house, after stopping our teams a hundred yards or so away, we saw a monstrous grizzly bear in a log cage. When much younger, he had been captured in the Rocky Mountains and brought all the way by the trappers down the Missouri River in a Mackinaw boat. Later on he was to be forwarded to St. Louis. It was the first live grizzly I had ever seen, and it was with no little caution that I drew near his cage to look at him. He must have weighed as much as seven or eight hundred pounds. His grizzly black fur was thick and glossy, his legs massive, and his great paws armed with long chisel claws. The ferocious beast soon became annoyed by our presence, though we kept a good two rods away from his cage. He uttered a loud growl, followed by a roar, and, rearing up, clawed at the side of his cage. This so startled both ourselves and our teams that we made haste to drive away.

We reached Hunsacker's ferry that evening.[15] Crossing over into Missouri, we continued on home. There was no other incident on the trip except that one day I had chills and fever in consequence of our camping among the malarial sloughs and drinking stagnant water while coming down the bottom road.

That August Father had been taken by an illness, which, in January 1844, finally proved fatal. He died at the age of forty-nine, by far the youngest of any of his forefathers or their wives since 1664. Even before we left Maine he had been feeble because of liver complaint, as it was called. His death was supposed to be due to this malady. It may, however, have been a result of medicine. It would seem he took enough of this to kill any man—for the most part big doses of calomel, rhubarb, and jalap—boluses, not pills. The theory then among physicians was to so reduce the system that the disease would have nothing on which to feed. Father was frequently bled. Towards the end, he was kept constantly under the influence of opium, prescribed by the doctor. The wonder is that he could have lived as long as he did under such treatment. He endured his suffering with great patience and died expressing his faith in the final redemption of all mankind. In those days that was regarded as extreme liberality of thought.

In January, shortly after Father's death, it became necessary for me, then a boy of seventeen, to go to the agency at Bellevue for the pay due my brother Isiah as the government blacksmith. The amount totaled $240, which in our section of the country was then a great amount of money. Cows were worth $5 or $6 apiece, horses from $20 to $25, dressed meats $1.50 a hundred pounds and about everything else in proportion.

I started from home January 12, on a cold, windy day. Mother had filled my saddlebags with an abundant supply of biscuits and boiled pork sausage. After crossing the Nodaway, I reached a stopping place that night about twenty miles from home. The next day I took an early start. But a little before sundown, while crossing Rock Creek, I let my horse drink heartily of the cold water. Overnight I stopped at Conrad Cliffield's in Linden, the county town.

Come morning, I found my horse badly foundered from the water he had drunk at Rock Creek. After treating and rubbing him an hour or so, I started on my way, which led across a cold prairie. Leading my poor horse, I walked until, about sundown, we got to McKissick's grove. Here I put up with Dan McKissick, who, though a stranger to me, had known my father. During the evening I made arrangements with him for a little mule on which to continue my journey. My horse was to remain in McKissick's care until my return.

In the morning I mounted the little mule—my saddle and saddlebags nigh covering him, and set off boldly. McKissick had instructed me to cross the river at Hunsacker's ferry and then turn to the left and take a trail along the bluffs that led to Major Cooper's. He said the mule knew the way and would readily follow the dim trail from the ferry.

So, with a spur on one heel and a rawhide quirt in my hand, and the biscuit and sausage lunch still untouched, I struck out.

McKissick had told me the truth. The little mule knew the way. After a quick journey of some fifteen miles, I reached Major Cooper's place. There I was to inquire of the major the best trail to take at that cold time of year to avoid Wabonsee [Waubansee] Lake and cover the thirty miles to reach Smith's place, the first house beyond Cooper's. With the desired information, I started on. But my mule showed a strong inclination against going any farther north. I had to use the spur and rawhide whip very freely to get him along at a tolerable pace.

About five miles above Major Cooper's we came to the crossing of a small creek. The stream had been swollen by rains, and, the weather turning suddenly cold, the water as it fell again had left ice on the banks and also a thin skin of ice on the running water. I rode down the bank, urging my mule forward with no little trouble. He went cautiously and reluctantly until his forefeet struck the ice hanging on the bank. At that he took fright. In spite of my efforts, he wheeled in the narrow train and went back up the bank. With my utmost urging, I could not force him down again.

Despairing to make him cross, it occurred to me that the stream probably spread over the low bottomlands a mile or two farther down. I might be able to cross there. My theory was right. But the water had flooded mud and grassland and had left ice on the grass as the creek shrank. This ice was an even greater terror to the mule than that up at the trail crossing. I could not make him face it. Greatly discouraged over the failure, I started back to the trail, intending to return to Major Cooper's and wait for company before again attempting to go on.

But before reaching the trail I saw a man on horseback about two miles away, coming from Cooper's. Whether it was a white man or Indian did not matter to me; either would be company and suit my purpose. My mule also saw and wanted to go to him. But I waited. The man, who was riding a large, bald-faced, sorrel horse, proved to be white. He said he had been hurrying to overtake me, as the trail was strange to him and he wanted to go through to the Indian mill, which was some three miles beyond what was then called Indian Hollow. The Hollow was afterwards named Council Bluffs—which name, by the way, was successively given to three different localities.

We at once started forward on the trail, he taking the lead. There was now no question of balking by the mule. He kept close to the horse's heels as the man rode down the bank at the creek crossing.

Though trembling with fear, the little mule still kept close behind, across the ford and up the far bank. A mile or so beyond the crossing, our trail turned sharply to the right, up into the hills to the east of Waubansee Lake, which lay close under the bluff and stretched for a mile or so out into the bottom. This turn altered the proper direction we ought to go, some forty-five or fifty degrees away from the place we wished to reach. Greatly nonplussed, we went down to the lake. It seemed to be hard frozen, and my companion said he thought the ice strong enough to bear his horses. I knew that if this was so, I and my mule could safely follow.

The crossing was made without mishap, and the risk was more than made up by the fun we had over the efforts of the mule to keep at the horse's tail. The horse was shod all around. But the mule was sharp shod only before, while his hind hoofs were bare. Part of the way across the lake he advanced on all fours, and then his hind feet would slip forward under him. He would come down on his hindquarters, walking in front and sliding behind on the glare ice.

That night we put up at Le Flambois's place, about ten miles beyond Smith's. Our mounts were stabled separately in rude cribs some distance apart, the doors being fastened with crisscross rails.

Le Flambois was a large, fine-looking French and Indian half-breed and son-in-law of the old Potawatomi chief Waubansee. The chief's wigwam was in the Waubansee Hills ten miles away. He was now here, visiting his son-in-law. All evening he sat with his squaw on a heap of buffalo robes and blankets on the floor in the middle of the room. After supper of corn pone and fried venison, which my companion and I had in the kitchen, we returned to the room where the others were seated. After talking over our trip and plans with Le Flambois, he told us that the Indian was Waubansee.

The old chief was bent and wrinkled, and appeared very decrepit. Most of the time he was half asleep. But during the course of the evening, with Le Flambois acting as interpreter, he told us in a feeble voice that he had been with Tecumseh and had fought Harrison's army at Tippecanoe. He went on to say that now his heart was very different, that he was glad to sleep in peace with the white man.

Next morning I found that my mule had crawled out of his stall through a very small opening and was standing at the other stall as near as he could get to the sorrel horse. When Le Flambois came into our room, he greeted me: "Well, le capitan, how you sleep las' ni'? I hope you sleep well." When I told him I had, he added: "Was that your mule? He make big noise las' ni'. I guess he 'fraid he lose his pony frien'. Maybe he not like Indian smell. He call very loud, many times." The mule had brayed nearly all night and, I fear, had kept the poor Frenchman awake.

By noon that day we reached Traders' Point (then called Council Bluffs) on the opposite side of the river from Bellevue.[16] This was virtually the end of my journey, as the agency was only about a mile away across the Missouri. So my mule had perforce to part company with his sorrel friend, whose rider rode on to the Indian mill. Risking again the dangerous crossing on the ice, I came safely to the agency and collected in gold the $240 due my brother from the government. Isiah was still at the missionary station up on the Loup Fork of the Platte River, ninety miles west.

When I was putting the gold in the rude money-belt that Mother had made for me before my start from home, Major Miller said: "Young man, you want to be pretty careful not to let anyone know your business here, or that you have money with you. If you do, those horse thieves and ruffians on the Hichinbodens above Hunsacker's ferry may take you in." This gave me no little concern, and it made me desirous of having the sorrel horse and his rider with me on my return. So I recrossed the river afoot and, saddling up my little mule, started for the Indian mill to find them. It was a good half day's ride, for the mill was situated about three miles beyond what is now called Council Bluffs on Mosquito Creek.

Reaching the mill at dark, I learned that my late companion had gone farther on into the country in search of the man with whom he had business. After stopping over for the night and until nearly noon the next day, the man returned. But it was with the news that he would not be able to conclude his business for two or three days more, perhaps longer. This was a great disappointment to me. However, while talking it over, a half-breed informed me that he had attended an Indian dance that night at the Hollow. There he had met a party of eight or ten Frenchmen and Indians who had come from a point twenty-five or thirty miles down the river. They were now about starting for home. Two of them would start for Smith's next morning at a very early hour, on a trip to Canada, in order to reach Fafa's ferry, forty-five miles away, by night.

This information gave me such spirit and courage that I at once mounted my mule and started over past the Hollow to overtake the returning party. After some four or five miles on my way, I espied the

French and Indian party. They were traveling at a lively rate on a parallel trail two miles ahead. At sight of them my stubborn mule needed no more urging with spur and whip. He raced forward. When we came up, I spoke with one of the Frenchmen. As soon as I told him where I was going, and that my mule would not travel well without company, he said, "Well, you stay with us. We give you good ride when you with us."

One of the party was a half-breed girl, who, I imagine, must have been the belle of the ball the previous night. She was all fixed up in wraps of many bright colors and was mounted on a handsome, gaily caparisoned dapple-gray pony with an Indian braid bridle and bonny sidesaddle. Her place was in the lead, and she set the pace at a lively hand-gallop. But my little mule was equal to the occasion. He kept up with the best of the ponies. At Smith's, which we reached at sundown, our gay girl leader turned aside to her own wigwam. That was the last I saw of her. She was pretty enough to have been Minnehaha.

At Smith's some of us stayed all night. We dined and breakfasted on "corn pone and hog meat," and I slept on the cabin floor wrapped in one blanket. Before daylight next morning, the little Frenchman, one of the half-breeds, and myself took an early breakfast. At sunrise we started off in the crisp cold, they on sharp-shod ponies, I on my half-shod mule. For the first five miles or more little was said, and I, a boy on my first trip alone from home, felt rather uneasy. I could not help wondering what sort of men my companions were, and if they were likely to surmise I had money with me. But, hit or miss, I was in for it, and on we went, my mule in much better spirits than myself.

After a time we came to a deep slough about thirty feet across. As at that creek crossing, it had been frozen when full, and the water then receding, the ice had sunk down about three feet in the center, making a trough. The sharp-shod ponies crossed over this without losing their feet. It was otherwise with my mule. When he started to follow, his hind feet slipped on the glare ice of the slope. Down he went, sliding behind and walking before, as at the creek crossing. After much slipping and struggling he carried me safe over and up the farther bank, where my two companions waited on their ponies, convulsed with laughter.

This little happening broke the ice, so to speak, and made us very sociable during the rest of our journey. After crossing another slough we turned aside, about one o'clock, into the long grass, to a pool of water a few yards down the trail. Here I opened my cold lunch of bread, butter, and boiled pork sausage, which we all greatly enjoyed.

About dark we reached the Nishnabotna and crossed over on Fafa's ferry. My companions were to stay overnight with Fafa. My own purpose was to cut across the hills some four miles to McKissick's place. It was quite dusk when I inquired the way of Fafa. He said: "You take dat trail you see. You go in it, ze mule he take you." So I gave the mule a loose rein, and he covered that four miles in about twenty minutes. He was on the home stretch, and now a winner.

When we drew near to the house, he announced our approach by a loud bray. The door was at once thrown open and I could see the interior full of light from a blazing hardwood fire in the big fireplace. I was very tired and cold, and the warm bright welcome I received made me supremely happy. With all the money I carried, it was a great relief to find myself safe back so near home. I was still further delighted to learn at supper that my foundered horse was quite sound again. After a good night's rest, I mounted my horse and rode off in high spirits. I reached home the evening of the second day after what to me had been a decidedly adventurous trip.

CHAPTER FIVE

Education 1846-1851

THAT SPRING of 1844 my brother Elisha went to visit our uncle, William Bennet, at Marietta, Ohio. When he returned in June he opened a subscription school for the neighborhood, the charge being $1.50 per scholar for a three-months' term. Early the next month, my brother John married Susan Anne Pittijohn, the daughter of a neighboring farmer. She was fifteen years old, and John was twenty-three. I took my best girl to the wedding on my old plow horse, Charlie, she behind on a blanket and I before on a borrowed saddle wearing my first "store clothes," a suit of Kentucky jeans. At the ceremony we stood up with the couple, I as best man and my girl as bridesmaid. Afterwards, we danced all night until broad daylight, when I took my girl home the same way we had come.

John had taught school for two winters, 1843 and 1844; also the spelling "schools," which were held on all weeknights. Those, together with the Sunday school meetings every Sunday and an occasional preaching by ministers of different denominations made up our chief amusements and recreations. The camp meetings, which usually were held during August and September every year, were great occasions for us. At such times, I and the other country boys enjoyed ourselves very much. I never "got religion," but nonetheless enjoyed seeing conversions.

On one occasion, at a camp meeting in the woods on Hackberry Ridge, there was great excitement. Ten or fifteen persons were "mourners" at the bench, shouting and groaning. I saw a colored woman start to climb a sapling that stood in what we boys called the bullpen—the space around the mourner's bench. She was screaming and crying that she "saw the Lawd up dat tree, shoo, and I's gwine for to git Him." And would you believe it, we just stood there and laughed.

The crop season of 1844 was unusually wet. In consequence my brother John and I, who were running the farm, raised little corn or wheat. However, we saved a late crop of buckwheat, of which we harvested about four hundred bushels. This, with such prairie chickens we could kill, was the substance of our living for the next twelve months.

During the last two or three years of my life on the farm, I would see the circuit judge and the lawyers passing through our lane on their way to hold court up in the northern counties of the circuit. They were well dressed in "store clothes" and rode good horses. What few law books they used they carried in their saddlebags. As before noted, our road, known as Bennet's Lane, was, I believe, the muddiest lane in the state of Missouri. Many a day I put in digging the road to make it passable, and I regret to say that I splattered mud on the back of more than one town "gent" who sneered down at me as he passed. Sight of the judge and lawyers riding by in their fine clothes, while I stood beside the road with my two linen sleeves rolled up and begrimed all over with dirt, made me draw rather bitter comparisons between my own existence and what I thought to be so easy and respectable a life.

This worked upon me until the fall of 1845. Then, on a cold, rainy November day while brother John and I were husking corn between the cribs, I found myself thinking I could not much longer bear such clodhopper drudgery year after year. I resolved that I would not endure it much longer. I told my brother I would work another year, get all the money I could by selling all my loose property, and go back to Ohio to get an education. I would then come home, teach school, study law, and become a lawyer. Brother John said, "Good enough."

Thenceforth I stuck to this resolution through thick and thin, though the next summer I came very near to throwing it up and enlisting in a company of volunteers that was being raised at Savannah, the county seat, to join Colonel [Alexander W.] Doniphan's command for the Mexican War. I was in the line of applicants, with only three ahead of me, when Isiah, my oldest brother, pulled me out. He said that before I enlisted he wanted me to talk with our mother. When I was home, she persuaded me to give up the idea of enlisting and to hold to my purpose of acquiring an education.

In August of that year, 1846, I sold three yoke of oxen at $28 a yoke and two nice young cavalry horses at Fort Leavenworth for $55 each. These were bought to outfit the command of Colonel Doniphan. The transaction gave me sufficient money to pay off my debts with $120 left, all in foreign gold, to provide for my trip and school expenses. I left home shabbily dressed. Isiah drove me and James Snuffin in our wagon to Weston. After waiting there some days for a boat, James and I bargained for deck passage to St. Louis on the steamer *Algoma*. We paid $2.50 each for a "red ticket," which required us to help the deck hands "wood" the steamer. Coal was not procurable nor used on that boat.

With such dock passage, you provided your own grub and blankets. A fellow deck passenger with his wife and children was a man named Benton—a poor relation (brother) of the great U. S. senator, Thomas [Hart] Benton. Never before had I known such a jolly devil-may-care fellow, so lively and entertaining with songs, jokes, and stories. One song was the then very popular "Spotted Fawn." This so captivated me that I learned to sing all its several verses. Another very different song, which must have come from the Georgia mountains, was a mock-tragic ditty tuned to a plaintive air. It was called the "Pisnous Sarpint." Here are the verses as I recall them after over sixty years:

On Kenesaw Mountain there did dwell
A lovely youth I knew full well, singing
Tu nic I da li tu di na di
Tu nic I da li tu di da.

This lovely youth one morn did go
Down in the medder all for to mow, singing
Tu nic, etc.

He had not mowed half 'round the field
Till a pizen sarpint bit his heel, singing
Tu nic, etc.

His poor old dad was standing nigh
A sittin' under a white ash dry, singing
Tu nic, etc.

He picked him up and carried him home
And delivered him over to his old wife Josh [?], singing
Tu nic, etc.

"My dearest son, why did you go
Down in the medder all for to mow, singing
Tu nic, etc.

"My dearest man, I thought you knowed
'Twas Daddy's hay and it had to be mowed, singing
Tu nic, etc."

The young man died and gave up the ghost
And away to the dickens he did post, singing
Tu nic, etc.

Now all you boys this moral take
Avoid the bite of a pizen snake; singing
Tu nic, etc.

At St. Louis, which we safely reached after nine days' passage, we laid over for two days and looked around the old French city. I bought a few buffalo robes to take to Ohio and sell on speculation. This venture in business brought neither loss nor gain. I sold the robes for just what they cost me. From St. Louis James Snuffin and I took passage for Cincinnati on the steamer *Swatara.* The Ohio River was very low at the time. One night, about ten o'clock, the steamer stuck upon a rock. It came near to staving a hole in her bottom and sinking her. I was scared, for I could not swim. But after the alarm was over I learned that I could have waded ashore.

At Louisville, in company with many other passengers, I landed and walked up the bank to reembark above the rapids. On the way we stopped to see Porter, the Kentucky giant, as he was called. He was between seven and eight feet high—but was not too high to keep a low doggery [dugout?] by the wayside. He was certainly a very big man but was most ungainly built and ill-proportioned.

While in St. Louis I had purchased a razor and the other articles of a shaving kit, also a pair of Oregon Tweed trousers and a blue blanket coat. Until later, however, I continued to wear my dirty, ragged farm suit. But at a little tavern in Cincinnati, where we got a room, I at last shed my old clothes. After an economical bath in a small tin tub, I put on my new suit, the best clothes I had ever owned. There was no doubt in my mind that I looked very "scrumptious."

That evening Snuffin and I went aboard a canal boat. After sailing all night on the "raging canawl," we reached a landing at Springville. There we stopped a day with Snuffin's uncle, Mr. Linell, a Universalist preacher. Next day we engaged a man to drive us over in his spring wagon to the farm of another of Snuffin's uncles, who lived near Woodstock, in Champaign County, Ohio. This uncle made us very welcome. But I was tired and sleepy, and at a very early hour retired to my bed, which was in the loft. The rain beating down on the roof above my head gave me a pleasant sense of comfort and security. I would have enjoyed it very much had I not been overtaken with a violent spell of homesickness. Though I was twenty years old, I must confess that I cried myself to sleep. The next day I walked into Woodstock to call upon Dr. Bowring and present a letter of introduction from his father-in-law, whom I knew in Missouri. After spending two days under the doctor's hospitable roof, he loaned me a horse to ride over into Crawford County, some sixty miles, and visit in the neighborhood of Galion, my boyhood home.

The first night out from Woodstock, I put up at a crossroads tavern in the beech woods. After a hearty supper and just before bedtime, mine host brought a large milk pan full of Bellafleur apples, the first I had ever seen. It was a great treat, for I had had little fruit in many years. After eating one of the apples with great relish, I was urged to take another. After eating this second one, I went to sleep in a big feather bed. About midnight I became aware that the landlord, after laying a door shutter on me, had climbed on top of it with a big butcher knife in his hand. He was trying to get at those apples I had eaten. Sleepless for the rest of the night, I rode away in the morning, too nauseated to eat any breakfast. About sundown I reached the town of Marion. There I stopped overnight with Squire Allen, to whom I had a letter of introduction from his brother-in-law, Captain Ashley. The captain lived near my home in Missouri and was the father of Isiah's wife, Clarissa.

Next even I stayed at the place of William H. Johnson, Father's journeyman blacksmith of former years. That night, wearing my new blanket coat, I went out with Johnson and his boys and dogs "coon" hunting. We returned after two or three hours' hunt, minus any "coons," but I brought back my coattails full of a kind of hard, little burrs called "beggar's lice." They were so small and so numerous that I never managed to get all of them out of my clothes. Still, there is no loss without some small gain. The burrs gave me employment for my fingers that winter when perplexed while reciting my grammar lessons to my teacher.

A few miles riding the next day brought me to the hospitable home of "Uncle Chauncey" Harding. He gave me a most cordial welcome. Then, seven years before, [when] I had left the neighborhood for the West, I was a small boy. Now I was a man grown, little short of six feet in height, and in consequence was quite a surprise to my old friends and schoolmates. My long blanket coat made a fine showing beside their homespun pink wammuses. I was lionized as though I were a great foreign gentleman. Invitations were given me to the corn huskings, apple cuttings, and other like social occasions all over the neighborhood. I was in great demand to carve the turkey at the hospitable tables spread for these gatherings.

After arranging for board for the winter at old "Grandfather" Story's at the rate of fifty cents a week, I borrowed Chauncey Harding's horse and open buggy and returned the horse loaned to me by Dr. Bowring at Woodstock. On my trip back I brought my buffalo robes and what little else baggage I possessed.

Early in that November of 1846 James Reeves, a Free-will Baptist, opened a private school in the Baptist church. This I attended for five months, every day except Sundays. Having had no schooling for seven years, other than our spelling contests, my education was very limited. Many of my former schoolmates shared Reeves's tuition with me. But they were all much advanced in their studies. My study of arithmetic had never gone beyond long division, and I knew nothing about grammar. I could not have told the difference between a noun and a verb. However, I had come to school to learn, and learn I did. Before the end of that five months, I had gone through *Kirkham's Grammar* and could parse as well as any of my schoolmates or even my teacher. My advance in arithmetic was less rapid, but I managed to plod through to the miscellaneous complicated examples at the end of *Adam's Arithmetic*

One or two, and sometimes even three times a week, we had spelling and singing schools. These were semi-social affairs such as "apple cuts" that included, along with the serious business of the evening, much eating of apples, also "sparking" and escorting the girls, often through the rain and snow and mud. A warm, hearty hospitality was the prevailing spirit of the community. There was one place I was always sure of an extra cordial welcome—the Hardings. There as a rule I had the pleasure of singing my favorite hymns, set to buckwheat notes in the "Missouri Harmony." This was in company with "Uncle" Chauncey, who led the singers at church. It was usual in those days for the minister to read the hymn through, then begin and read a verse. The singers would sing it. He would read the next verse, which they would sing, and so on until the hymn was completed in alternate installments. The entire congregation joined in the service. This was Free Baptist.

There were four boys in the Harding family—Nehemiah, Horace, Jotham, and Amos—the oldest of them five years my junior. It afterwards transpired that all of them, with the exception of Jotham, were so impressed by my remarkable travels and high ambitions that they likewise left the home farm and went out in search of broader fields of action. Nehemiah took up the book business in Cincinnati. Horace, after learning the printer's trade, studied law and afterwards became my first law partner out in western Iowa. Amos, the youngest, joined the volunteers in 1861 and during the war became judge advocate in the Department of Missouri at St. Louis. After the war he and Nehemiah went into the insurance business, in which they were very successful.

Following the close of our winter's school term at the Baptist church, Nehemiah and I attended school at a little academy in Marion, Ohio. Before the third month ended, however, the principal of this school became so dissipated that the academy was closed. Nehemiah returned home, but I remained at Marion, studying alone at my boardinghouse until my funds ran low. On applying for work from my old friend, William Johnson, he engaged me for a month on his farm during harvest time and paid me with a ten-dollar order for store goods. By means of this order, I obtained a coat of farmer's satin and a pair of stylishly cut striped trousers.

The following September, 1847, Miles Hosford, his sister Becky, his cousin Phoebe, Nehemiah Harding, and myself went down to a little town called Amalthea, twelve miles from Columbus. There we attended Central College. I cut wood and rang the chapel bell to pay board and tuition. By Christmas I had made much headway in my studies, but my money was all spent. Shortly before this, a number of the students had indulged in so much fun and horseplay that many of them were now expelled by the faculty. Truth to tell, I and Miles Hosford had been among the most mischievous. Feeling that we too might be expelled, we persuaded all of our little party to quit school and go back home with us.

Upon our return to Galion, I endeavored to replenish my purse by teaching a subscription school of my own. It is no more than fair to myself to relate that I made more of a success with my teaching than in collecting the subscriptions. During the term of my school, we were bantered to a spelling contest by a larger school in the neighborhood taught by a young lady. They were determined to defeat not only my school but its teacher also. We met them at their schoolhouse one winter night in February, and "Uncle" Jimmy Dunlap was chosen to pronounce, that is, "give out the words." Two sets of scholars, each with its teacher at the head, ranged themselves on the opposite sides of the room, and at it we went.

Among my pupils were only three or four good spellers, while the other side could count upon twelve or fifteen. A few rounds of spelling reduced the contestants to those numbers. The contest now waxed warm, with every prospect of victory for our opponents. After five or six rounds, all my following were downed. I was left alone to face the other teacher, backed by five of her best pupils. The next number on their program was to take my scalp.

Great as was my danger, I managed to keep cool and determined to win. I realized that the reputation of my school now depended solely upon myself. There was much excited spelling on both sides. Very soon we two teachers were left standing alone. That seemed to make the young lady overeager and, as I was pleased to note, rather nervous. Whenever it came her turn she would snap at the word as soon as pronounced, and spell it quickly. I was more deliberate, spelling slowly and smiling across at my opponent. She became more and more flustered and hasty, and at last misspelled a simple word that she well knew. Quick as a flash I spelled it *right*, putting her down and out, and my scholars fell to cheering and clapping.

When I sat down, with as much modesty as I could assume after so notable a victory, someone suggested that I should get up alone and continue spelling until I missed. I declined on the plea that such a proceeding would be apt to keep them up too late. This spelling contest was the talk of the neighborhood for the rest of the winter. It helped me not a little to collect enough of my subscriptions to carry me back home the following May.

The main event of my return to Missouri was the train ride from Xenia, Ohio, to Springfield. It was the first time I had journeyed by railroad. That method of travel was then much more hazardous for passengers than it is now, though the average speed was not much greater than six to eight miles an hour. The greatest danger lay in the rails, which were nothing more than bars of strap iron, not fastened on cross ties, as at present, but on square timbers laid lengthwise with them. Now and then a rail would break. The broken end, which was called a "snake head," like as not would tear its way up through the floor of a car to wreak havoc among the seats and the legs of unlucky passengers. These iron "snake heads" were more to be dreaded than the most poisonous of the snake family. However, I escaped this danger, as well as all others.

My summer at home was spent in an earnest endeavor to find the means to return to school. One chance was a loan of money from my oldest brother, Isiah. To this purpose, I borrowed a horse and heavy buggy from Warren Samuels in Savannah and took Mother the hundred-mile journey to Bellevue. Isiah was now living there with his family and still employed as a blacksmith at good pay by the government.

This Indian country, as I have told, belonged to the Omaha tribe. Indians were numerous around the agency. They filled the air with a strong odor of smoked skins and filth peculiar to all Indians and known as the "Indian smell." This was new and strange to my horse. It made him nervous all the time we remained there.

On a Sunday morning after we reached my brother's house, we hitched up the horse to the buggy for a ride. I drove, with Mother and Clarissa, Isiah's wife, beside me on the seat. In my lap I had my brother's daughter Maria, then between two and three years old, holding her with my left hand and the reins in my right. Clarissa sat on the other side, holding Melissa, then a baby. Mother was between us.

As the road was smooth and level, Isiah and John Snuffin sat on the back end of the box with their feet hanging down outside. We had to pass through a lane with a square turn in it. A short distance before reaching this turn we were quietly proceeding, with our horse at a walk. But just as we were opposite a wigwam, an Indian suddenly came out of it and shook a buffalo robe, I suppose to get off the dust. Greatly startled, our horse threw up his head and bolted off in great fright. He raced along the lane between the high rail fences on either side towards that square turn. As I was holding little Maria in one hand, I could not gather up the lines to stop the horse. Yet I had to do something before we got to that sharp turn. I dropped one line and with the other pulled the horse right into the fence.

It was a Virginia fence made with cottonwood rails. The horse struck it hard, knocking down two panels. He went down also, breaking off one of the thills, or shafts, of the buggy. Clarissa, Mother, and I and the two children were pitched out at the horse's heels, under the wheels. Before he could get up to start again, Isiah and John Snuffin ran around from behind to grab him by the head. They held him fast until we all got out of the wreck. None of us were in the least hurt, but all were greatly scared, especially poor, dear old Mother. She did not get over her fear of the horse running away again all during our journey back home to Missouri.

Isiah mended the broken buggy nicely, and afterwards, whenever I hitched up the horse, I fastened a martingale to the bridle bits. With this extended between his forelegs to the bellyband, he could not throw up his head to run away. If he started to do so, as he did fifty times before we reached home, I was on the watch for him. With his head held down and both my hands on the lines, I could hold him under safe control. It was Mother's first outing from home since leaving Ohio in 1839. So the visit was a memorable one to her and she greatly enjoyed it, notwithstanding that runaway horse. Also, Isiah had loaned me forty dollars to aid my return to school.

By fall I found myself the possessor of two horses and enough money to pay my expenses overland to Ohio. It was a journey of more than eight hundred miles, but I covered it on horseback without much fatigue or difficulty, alternately riding one of my horses and leading the other. On the last day of my trip I reached Mount Gilead, Ohio, in time to hear Thomas Gorwin make a "stump" speech in favor of the election of old "Zack" Taylor for president. It was one of the best stump speeches I have ever heard. At this meeting I chanced upon the Hardings, who had come down to attend it. That night I accompanied them to their hospitable home some twelve miles away.

After "recruiting" my jaded horses for a few weeks, I traded one of them to a storekeeper for clothing. Then, one cold, rainy day in November, accompanied by my kind benefactor, "Uncle Chauncey" Harding, I rode the other horse over to Delaware, Ohio. There I traded the animal to the proprietor of the Hinton House for board.

Without delay, I took up a special course of study at the Ohio Wesleyan University at Delaware. My intention was to take the full three courses at the university and graduate. But, much to my sorrow, at the end of four months, sickness compelled me to abandon the entire project. During my illness, which lasted for several weeks, my funds ran low. I sent to my brothers in Missouri for money, but they could spare me no more than twenty dollars. This came in the form of a Missouri bank bill, which, though as good as gold, barely sufficed to pay up some balances that I owed.

One warm March day, still feeble from my sickness, I was sitting in the public room of the hotel brooding over my forlorn condition when my attention was attracted by the talk of two men nearby. One of them stated that he intended to start overland for California in a short time. He inquired of the other as to the best plan for outfitting on the Missouri before beginning the trip across the plains. When the other man said he knew nothing about the matter, I saw my chance. I knew all about it, for St. Joe was the best place for outfitting, and St. Joe was all but next door to the home to which I was so anxious to return.

I at once moved my chair around and gave the desired information to the man. While doing so, I had the good fortune to recognize him as George Rowe, one of my boyhood Ohio teachers. At this time he was an attorney-at-law of Marion, Ohio. When I gave my name, he remembered me in turn. Inside of an hour I was seated beside him in his buggy on the way to Marion. Two weeks later he started from Marion for the West with two wagons and four horses and accompanied by myself and three other hired men. I had entered into an agreement to pay him for my fare on reaching my home.

At Cincinnati we boarded a steamer—wagons, horses, and all—and traveled by water to St. Louis. While laying over there for a Missouri River boat, we heard a startling account of the prevalence of cholera on the river. This made Mr. Rowe somewhat nervous. Yet we boarded the first steamer that started for St. Joe. Mr. Rowe took a stateroom. The other men and myself found good quarters in the wagon beds on the hurricane deck. In view of the cholera news, I had brought aboard with me *The Border Beagles,* a very exciting story of love and adventure in Arkansas and southeast Missouri.

About eleven o'clock, on the second night out from St. Louis, we buried one of the deck passengers who had died of cholera. Others on the lower deck were sick with the terrible disease. Next day at St. Charles we sent ashore another corpse. Late in the afternoon of the third day, Mr. Rowe sent for me to come to his stateroom. I divined at once that he had been taken with the cholera. Holding fast to my "yellowback" *Border Beagles,* I went down into the cabin to his room. I was not mistaken. He looked like a very sick man, and the doctor said he had the cholera.

When I came to his bedside, Mr. Rowe expressed no little concern over his condition. He spoke of dying and began to give me directions about his business. I tried to cheer him up by asserting that he need not die unless he wanted to, and by assuring him that I would stay with him until he recovered. Then I took a seat beside the door of his stateroom, where I could see him and be near to wait on him, and at the same time read my *Border Beagles* by the light of the chandelier in the corridor. At regular intervals I gave him medicine as directed by the doctor.

All that night—a very long one to me—I stayed at my post, without a wink of sleep, going in every few minutes to wait upon the sick man. The doctor called every half hour until he said to me that my friend had passed the crisis. By seven the next morning he was much better.

He was quite a fleshy man, but that one night made a big reduction in his weight.

For my part, I not only gained a good appetite for breakfast by my night's work but also the favor of Mr. Rowe. On regain[ing] his feet, he dubbed me "Don Hiram," and when we came to St. Joe he refused to take a cent for bringing me home from Ohio. Moreover, he wished me to go with him to California and promised that the trip should cost me nothing. When I told him of my intention to read law, he said that his law library was to be shipped to California by water and that when we got there I should study law in his office, free of charge. Had it not been for my mother's desire for me to remain with her, I should have accepted this generous offer. But her love far outweighed Mr. Rowe's gratitude and friendship. So I stayed at home and taught school.

While in Ohio I had read much of Shakespeare. Now, while teaching school in 1850 and 1851, I read Burns, Byron, and Bailey's poem "Festus." From the latter I got great insight of life and gratification of mind and soul—greater than all the other poems that I read in early life. Byron was one of my favorites. I found his Hebrew melodies particularly enjoyable. But I only admired him. I read little of Pope yet enough to form an opinion that in *insight* he is the peer of any of the great poets. Burns was the one above all whom I loved, with a joy that has lasted all the many years since I read his poems for the first time.

At night I read law, much of the time by firelight. The books I studied were borrowed from lawyers in Savannah, most of them from Prince L. Hudgens. In May 1851 I was admitted to the bar by Thomas S. Leonard, then judge of that circuit.

CHAPTER SIX

Law and Politics 1852-1854

SHORTLY after my admission to the bar, I was called to my first case. It was before a justice of the peace on Round Prairie in Andrew County. Just how the trial resulted has slipped my memory. I am inclined to believe that I lost the case. However, I received a small fee and must have made some reputation in the conduct of the suit, for before leaving the neighborhood I was entrusted with the collection of a note for $800. The claim was against old Joe Hunter of my own county. The note had been given by him in payment for a Negro slave whom he had bought of the Currier estate.

I brought suit in the circuit court, which met in September. The case was set for trial while I was home sick with the chills and fever. The news that it was to be held the following day came to me when I was too sick to leave my bed. Notwithstanding my condition, I would have made an effort to attend court had not my informant added that General Alexander W. Doniphan had been retained by Hunter. At this what little strength I had immediately vanished. General Doniphan, who had served in the Mexican War, was one of the best lawyers in the state of Missouri.

Though I was careful not to say so at the time, I must confess I was even more pleased to be too sick to attend that trial than I had been over the attack of measles in harvest time during my childhood days back in Ohio. Much to my surprise and gratification, I won my case, or it won itself, while I was four miles away from the courthouse. When, after court adjourned, I went to town, I was told that Doniphan had looked over the papers which I had prepared and said that they were all right. Then, after examining the note, he had told his client to pay the debt, as he had no defense against it. Without doubt Doniphan would have been no less considerate of me than of my papers, had I been present in my first case of record. He was a big, generous, kind-hearted man.

Soon after this I sold my land, a hundred acres, which had been part of the old farm. Then for the second time, I scraped the Missouri mud off my feet. With what I could rake together of money and books, I went up to Mills County in western Iowa. This country, which I had "explored" in 1843 and 1844, had recently been purchased from the Potawatomi Indians. I bought from a Mormon a claim on the public land near Coonville, now Glenwood. A little later, after a trip back to Missouri, I put up my "shingle" in Coonville—being the only lawyer in town. My card in the one paper of the place read:

H. P. Bennet
Attorney at Law
References—got none.

The next spring, 1852, I married Sarah McCabe, the daughter of James B. McCabe of Glenwood. Owing to the interference of Sarah's stepmother, we made a runaway match. I secured a pair of saddle horses, and we rode some twenty miles over into the next county, where we were married by Judge Greenwood. Our marriage proved a most happy one. We had six children, the three oldest of whom, Isabel, Carrie, and Friel, died in infancy. Hiram, John, and Sara survived. Their mother died November 16, 1867, at Denver, Colorado.

Having preempted and entered the land claim that I had bought from the Mormon, I purchased a house and lot in Glenwood and moved into town. Early in that year, 1852, a vacancy occurred in the office of county judge through the resignation of the incumbent. Boy as I was and looked to be, I was elected to fill the vacancy. This, the first office I held, did not at all interfere with my law practice. On the contrary, it gave me some helpful notoriety and a touch of dignity. I held the judgeship until the fall of 1854, when I resigned and moved to Nebraska City.

As has been told, the Oto Indians inhabited the country in Nebraska west of the Missouri and south of the Platte. Their principal village, which was built of sod wigwams, was located about three miles west of what is now the site of Plattsmouth and some ten or twelve miles from Glenwood. During May 1854 a party of these Otoes came over to our side of the Platte and stole a great number of horses from the settlers. This they did so craftily that no one suspected them of being the thieves. For some time it was generally supposed that the horses had been stolen by white men.

The following August, while Judge A. A. Bradford[17] was holding a term of the district court at Glenwood, there came to court as a witness in one of the cases a man named Jim O'Neal. He kept a little store, principally of "wet groceries," on the side of the river opposite where Plattsmouth is now located. Just before starting back home, Jim gave out to one of the ranchmen whose horses had been stolen that some Otoes, among whom he named Louis Fafa, a half-breed, had been to his place two or three days past. They had offered, for a consideration, to return a lot of horses stolen by members of their tribe that spring. Jim said he thought he could get the horses at the rate of about five dollars a head.

After he left town, his story was quickly spread among the town people and neighboring farmers. It created no little feeling. Everyone at once became convinced that the Otoes were the thieves who had made off with all the horses stolen in May. A meeting was called, and within two hours a party of seventeen riders started from Glenwood for the Indian village across the river. The purpose was to retake the stolen animals. Many of the party were armed and were more disposed to give the Indians lead than to give them money through their go-between O'Neal.

Though I had lost no horses, I joined my neighbors, mounted on my fine little mare, Punkin. Ben Lambert rode beside me, still better mounted on a flea-bitten grey. In fact, all of the party were well mounted. When we came to the river, we had no means to get across other than Jim O'Neal's flatboat. It was large enough to take the men but not all the horses.

Among the five for which room was found on the first trip, Lambert and I managed to get our mounts included. We landed under the bluff at what is now the north part of the township of Plattsmouth. We hurried up the hill, from the top of which was a view of the little valley that extended from the river to a belt of timber. At the far side of the trees, three miles from the river, the Indian village was situated on the prairie.

Near the river we saw a single Indian walking in the direction of the village. Also, about halfway between him and the woods, an Indian boy on a pony was coming down the trail from the village. Both Indians saw our party at the same moment we sighted them. At a sign from the nearer buck, the boy whirled his pony about and raced back for the village at full speed. We started after him in hot haste, eager to catch him before he could reach and apprise the village of our coming. I took the lead on Punkin and easily kept it all up the valley until within a quarter mile of the village. The boy was only some seventy-five yards ahead of me when Ben Lambert came forging up beside me on his flea-bitten grey, yelling, as we all were, at the top of his voice.

Punkin did her best, but the grey finally passed her and got ahead into the narrow trail. On we raced at top speed. When we reached the village, Ben's horse was only a few jumps behind the pony of the little Indian, with Punkin and I close after. All three animals were well winded, for it was a hot day and they had been going their fastest.

The Indian boy did not stop his pony to dismount. He threw himself off at the entrance of the first wigwam and scrambled out of sight. Ben and I had left the other three horsemen far behind, while they had outridden the unmounted members of the party, who had hurried after us without waiting for their horses to be brought across the river.

The shouts of Ben and myself in our pursuit of the Indian boy had aroused the village. Before our three fellow horsemen came up, at least a hundred Indians were in sight. One of them, who I suppose was the village "crier," ran up on top of the sod council house and shouted something in the Oto language at the top of his lungs. We could not tell what he was saying until we saw eight or ten young fellows running from the village towards a band of some two or three hundred horses grazing on the prairie about a quarter mile away. It was easy to see the purpose of this, and having been joined by old Lewis Johnson and Nickelwait and the other mounted men, we galloped after the racing Indians.

By quick work, we managed to secure four large American horses before the young bucks could run the band into the brush and ravines, out of sight. With these four horses in hand, we returned to the village just as our infantry division of twelve came up. For a time there was great excitement and confusion until Louis Fafa put in an appearance. Fafa was a half-breed French and Indian who had received a good education in St. Louis and had lived among white people several years. But he had returned to the blanket state and was the most Indiany Indian and biggest thief in the tribe. He could talk English and French as well as Oto.

For the occasion, he came in well as interpreter and go-between. Feeling certain that he had been one of the Indian thieves who had stolen our horses in Iowa, we told him in pretty certain language that we had come for all those he and others of his tribe had taken and that we were going to get them now. Old Lewis Johnson, a desperate character, who at the time was half full of whiskey, did most of the talking for us. He had his pistol out and was very violent in his manner. In fact, it was a wonder that he did not shoot Louis Fafa—in which event the Indians would have cleaned us out of the village. There were three or four hundred of them, while our party, as I have said, numbered only seventeen, and we were only half armed with shotguns and pepperbox revolvers.

Fortunately, no blood was shed, and Fafa soon came to terms. He explained that some of the stolen horses were out on the Weeping Water ten miles away but that he would at once send for them. After three or four long hours of waiting, fifteen of our stolen horses were brought in and delivered over to us. With these we started home. Recrossing the river on the flatboat at sundown, we reached Glenwood at eleven o'clock, tired and hungry from our successful Indian raid. This was my first Indian campaign, in which, as I am glad to say, I neither fought, bled, nor died.

That same year, 1853, I was present at the negotiation of the Indian treaties at Bellevue, Nebraska, when the Omaha and Oto Indians sold their lands to the government. My oldest brother, Isiah, had returned to the government employ and was acting as gunsmith for these tribes.[18] But for him, I believe that at the time the Otoes would have refused to negotiate with the government agents.

When they first met in council some of the chiefs became very angry at others. And so many of the braves opposed treating that the council broke up, and all the Indians went back to their villages south of the Platte River. That night my brother was sent after them. After stopping at the villages a day or two, he brought back to Bellevue a delegation of chiefs empowered to settle the matter. With these there was soon concluded a satisfactory treaty for the sale of all the lands of the Otoes in southern Nebraska.

In the fall of 1854 I moved to Nebraska City in Otoe County. But before leaving Glenwood, I had laid claim to a quarter section on Papillion Creek about two miles southwest from the Presbyterian mission house at Bellevue in Sarpy County.[19] Isiah, who was still stationed at Bellevue in government employ, took a claim alongside mine. We soon turned over both claims to our brother, Joseph F. Bennet, who made his home on them for several years.

While I was still at Glenwood, Horace H. Harding came out from Ohio and joined me as a law partner, our firm name being "Bennet and Harding." A year after my move to Nebraska City, Harding followed me. About the same time, J. Sterling Morton joined our firm for a year or so, the name being, "Bennet, Morton, and Harding." Within a month or two after my move to Nebraska City, I was elected to the first territorial legislature of Nebraska as a member of the upper house, or council.[20] With little knowledge of parlimentary law and no previous experience in a legislative body, I was thrust into the chair as the temporary presiding officer to organize the council. My friends and fellow members from south of the Platte River were pledged to locate the capital of the territory at Plattsmouth. The secretary and acting governor, Thomas B. Cummings, had called the legislature to convene at Omaha, where he and all the members from north of the Platte wanted the capital permanently located.

After we were temporarily organized, Cummings sought to swear us in. When we all stood up, he pronounced the usual oath of office. He then continued with the words that we were each over the age of twenty-one years. I was standing beside Lafe Knuckolls of Cass County, south side of the Platte.[21] At once I dropped into my seat and pulled Lafe down with me. When Cummings got through, I denied that I had been sworn. The chief justice was then called in. He administered the oath again, leaving out the twenty-one-year clause. Off side, after Lafe and I had taken the oath, Cummings, in presence of all, laughingly asked him how old he was. Lafe replied, "Ask my constituents." Boy that he was, he made a good member and sat out the full term, without further question of his age.

The location of the capital was the all-absorbing one in the organization of both houses of the legislature. The south Platte members had a majority of one in the council, whereby I had been foistered [sic] into the chair at the opening of the first day's proceedings. My term of authority was brief. Before a permanent organization could be effected by our party, the Omaha advocates [brought] over to their side one of our men, J. L. Sharp, by an offer of the presidency of the council, together with a large block of stock in the Omaha Town Company.[22] Accordingly, Sharp was elected president of the council and received enough stock to have made him rich. The bill fixing the capital at Omaha was duly passed by his help and became a law. Likewise with his help, all other measures in which the north Platte party was interested were passed and settled.

But a day or two before final adjournment of the legislature, an Omaha man named Hanscom, who was president of the Omaha Town

Company, asked Sharp to turn over his stock to be countersigned and registered. Sharp fell into the trap and never again set eyes on his stock. We others of the south Platte party were not greatly grieved by his loss. The transaction soon became known among Sharp's constituents, and he never dared to show his face among them thereafter.

It had been contemplated by the friends who had induced me to resign my judgeship in Iowa and move to Nebraska City that I should stand for election as the first delegate in Congress from the territory of Nebraska. But owing to my lack of experience in political manipulations, I withdrew my candidacy at the instance [insistence] of Judge Holly and Napoleon B. Giddings in favor of the latter. He was elected after a brief canvass through the sparse settlements of the territory. The office would have been mine but for my weakness in yielding to the solicitations of Giddings and Holly. Though my friends were disgusted by my act, they at once put me on the ticket for councilman, and, as I have previously stated, elected me to the first legislature of Nebraska Territory.

For nearly a year after June 1854 both myself and my family were more or less passing to and fro between Glenwood, Iowa, and Nebraska City. But at last, in April 1855, we managed to get settled at the latter place in a small house which I built on a plot now called "The Elms." Speaking of that name reminds me that I planted those elms around my lots with some other trees in the latter part of March 1855. Small as they were, and of little note at the time, their shadows have never grown less. To the best of my knowledge, my tree planting was the first attempt of its kind in Nebraska City. It was suggested to me by what is said in *The Autocrat of the Breakfast Table* of the elms on Boston Common, "extending their wide arms, in attitude conferring a constant blessing on the people."[23] I like to flatter myself with the thought that this endeavor to improve the appearance of my home may have given J. Sterling Morton the germ of his idea of Arbor Day. To have contributed, even in the remotest degree, to the inauguration of such a beautiful and beneficial practice would afford any man just cause to be proud.

CHAPTER SEVEN

Washington Sojourn 1855-1856

IN 1855 my south Platte friends put me forward as a candidate to Congress to succeed Cummings. His term was only a fractional one. It ended March 4, when he went back home to Savannah, Missouri. My principal backer was Stephen F. Knuckolls, a wealthy merchant of Linden, Missouri, and of Sidney and Glenwood, Iowa.[24] He had been one of the first to buy the ground at old Fort Kearney and lay off the town of Nebraska City. I was also supported by my law partner, J. Sterling Morton, who was at the same time the editor of the *Nebraska City News.*

None of us knew just what to call ourselves politically. Nuckolls and I had been Whigs. Morton was a strong Democrat but did not like the Democratic territorial administration. In local politics the administration was "North Platte," and Morton, like the rest of us, was "South Platte." Accompanied part of the time by Morton, I took the stump and canvassed the territory as candidate for delegate to Congress. It goes without saying that south of the Platte I emphasized my position as an anti-administration candidate but when north of the Platte I ignored that question.

The returns showed a small vote with a majority in my favor of fifty-seven. The governor and canvassing board, however, threw out enough ballots to make a majority against me. They therefore gave the certificate of election to my opponent, Bird B. Chapman.[25] The latter had come out from Ohio to Nebraska to run for the office of delegate, just as Giddings the previous year had come out from Missouri. After his term of office expired, Chapman, like Giddings,[26] returned to his home in Ohio and never again, to the best of my knowledge, came back to Nebraska, even for a visit.

My friends advised me to contest Chapman's seat in Congress.[27] So, as I was now fairly in the political swim, I borrowed $600 from my brother John for my expenses and set out for Washington with my wife Sarah and little daughter Carrie. Capt. Jonathan Shinn drove us in a spring wagon behind a pair of good horses from Nebraska City to Ottuma [Ottumwa], Iowa.

By stage we continued our journey to Burlington. There, at night, I had a severe fall from the hotel veranda, an accident that came near to ending my career. It detained us for two days before I was able to travel. An account of it got into the papers and brought about a visit from Governor Grimes of Iowa.[28] While at Glenwood I had made his favorable acquaintance during his canvass for office by actively supporting and carrying for him Mills County, of which at the time I was county judge. The governor's call was noted in the papers, and quite a good send-off was given me personally and politically in the *Burlington Hawkeye*.

We continued on east to Galion, Ohio, where I had lived as a boy. There I left my wife and babe at the hospitable home of my old friend Asa Hosford and his wife while I went on alone, reaching Washington the latter part of November. This was my first trip to any place east of Ohio since my father emigrated with his family from Maine in 1831. Passing through Baltimore, the railroad cars were hauled across the city to the Washington depot by a string of large draft horses, hitched tandem. They were slow but sure. At Washington I put up for a day at the Dexter, a large hotel on Seventh Street near Pennsylvania Avenue. It was a high-toned place, of an elegant old-colonial style. John B. Crittenden, who was there with his family, was the most distinguished guest.[29] As a matter of fact, the place was altogether too high-toned for my financial circumstances. After one day, I went to the private boardinghouse of Mrs. Fitzgerald on Pennsylvania Avenue near 4½ Street. After a few weeks I moved again, this time to the Washington House. There, for two months, I sat opposite Sen. Hannibal Hamlin at the dinner table. Others at the same table were Rives, proprietor of the *Washington Globe*, and Rep. George W. Jones of Tennessee, "the great objector" and watchdog of the Treasury.

That winter of 1855–56, I became quite dudish, shaved my beard to a goatee, and frequently attended the theater, all alone except for a whiskey sour. It was the first time I had ever gone to theaters, and I enjoyed it more that winter than ever since. One reason for this may have been that Joe Jefferson was playing in a Washington stock company. I enjoyed him greatly, though it was four years later that he became known as a star of the first magnitude.

Meanwhile there had been great delay over the organization of the House of Representatives. The members had been called to order [at] twelve o'clock on the first Monday of December 1855. This took place in the old hall of the House, now the Hall of Statuary.[30] The new or present hall was not occupied until the opening of the Thirty-sixth Congress. After the roll call of the members, the clerk announced that the first business in order was the election of a Speaker. He then commenced to call the roll for the vote, each member voting for the nominee of his party. No election occurred on this first call, nor on the next or the next, .that first day. Nor was there any election thereafter, though the roll was called nearly every succeeding day until the third of February 1856.[31]

Then at last, by a rule adopted that morning for the purpose of securing an election, after five ballots the final voting resulted in the election of Nathaniel B. Banks as Speaker.[32] The total vote for him was less than a majority of the representatives. [With] knowledge of the rule adopted and [the realization] that it would result in the election of a Speaker before the day closed, the galleries and lobby were crowded with excited people, myself included.

When the final vote was announced, such yelling and hissing from the galleries that old hall never heard, before or since. After this subsided, the clerk appointed a committee of three—Howell Cobb, Robert Aiken, and Henry Full, all of whom had been opposing candidates—to conduct the Speaker-elect to the chair.[33] This being done, the oldest member, Joshua R. Giddings of Ohio, a large, venerable old man, stepped into the area in front of the Speaker's stand. With Mr. Banks standing up in his place, Giddings administered to him the oath of his office. Thereupon and before he took his seat, Mr. Banks lifted the gavel. At that, the mace, which is the emblem of authority in the House, was put in place by the acting sergeant at arms. The gavel fell and rapped to order, and at that moment the House of Representatives of the Thirty-fifth Congress was organized.[34]

Mr. Banks was the most dignified and perfect Speaker I ever saw preside in the House, or elsewhere, and I have seen a good many— Colfax, Blaine, Reed, and others.

Not until the House was fully organized could any member or officer or clerk connected with the House draw a cent of pay.[35] You may well imagine the relief this brought to everyone—members, officers, clerks, boardinghouse keepers, and indeed almost the entire community of the city. In a few days the committees were announced, and they soon got to work preparing the business of the session.

When first reaching Washington, I had made the acquaintance of a Mr. Weston of Maine and had employed him as my attorney on a contingent fee of $300 if I won my seat. My choice of him was due to the fact that he had given me a favorable introduction to the three Washburn brothers then in Congress. Israel Washburn, Jr., was the member from the district in Maine in which I was born. My introduction to him was particularly fortunate, as he was made chairman of the House Committee on Elections upon the organization of the House in February.

In April I sent to Ohio for my wife and child. They got through safely, and I met them in Baltimore. We boarded and roomed at Mrs. Washington's, a brick house on Capitol Hill, north of the Capitol. This place had once been occupied by Henry Clay. Like several others in the neighborhood, it was among the very first built in the city—one of them by George Washington. About 1875, during Boss Shepperd's administration, all these houses were torn down to make room for the extension of the Capitol grounds northwards. In 1856 the new Senate and new House wings of the Capitol building were well along towards completion. They were occupied by Congress in 1858.

When in April the Election Committee made its report, my contest against Chapman was decided in my favor.[36] But owing to the dilatoriness of Cooper K. Watson, the committee member who had written up and had charge of the matter, the report was not called up for action by the House until the twenty-fourth of July. Had it been more prompt, I believe that I would certainly have been seated.

During the delay, J. S. Sharp, of Omaha stock fame, came on to Washington in the interest of Chapman. With him he brought four *ex parte* affidavits from persons in Nebraska who were my political enemies. These affidavits were handed to Alexander H. Stevens, a member of the Election Committee. I was informed that he, without submitting them to the committee, made them the basis of a majority report against me. Until the Stevens report was printed, I neither saw nor knew of the existence of the affidavits. Notwithstanding all this, I believe I would yet have won my contest had not Watson delayed action until after the Republican convention in Philadelphia.

This convention was held in June 1856, and I went over to see how a great convention was conducted. During the few months that I had been lobbying to gain the seat against Chapman, I had acquired knowledge that had made [me] more than ever an anti-administration man—to realize that I was, in fact, a Republican. The convention met and at once organized by electing as president Henry S. Lane of Indiana, a Henry Clay Whig. A motion was then made to give every state and territory a vice-president. I was standing on a seat in the crowd at the very back of the hall when a member of Congress who knew about my contest against Chapman came to me and asked me to become one of the vice-presidents of the convention. Upon my reply that I was not a delegate, he said there was none whatever from Nebraska. But as it was desired that a showing be made from all the states and territories, the convention would recognize me as delegate from Nebraska if I would consent to act. At this I consented willing enough and so had the honor of sitting on the stage in company with all the other vice-presidents at the first national convention of the Republican party. It was a step I have never regretted, although I am satisfied that when my contest against Chapman came to a vote in the House, I was defeated solely because I had become known as a notorious "Black" Republican.

In the House that had elected N. P. Banks [as] Speaker, there were three parties: the Democratic, the American, and the Republican. The first and second were fully organized; the last was just forming, and its first victory was the election of Banks by a plurality. The northern members of the American party were inclined towards the Free Soil movement; and all of them, north and south, were as much opposed to President Pierce's administration as were the members of the new, half-formed Republican party. Hence, as long as I had been rated merely as an anti-administration man, I had had the promised support of many of the American members. Among those who had said they would give me their votes were Henry Winter Davis, Solomon G. Davis,[37] and John S. Carlile of West Virginia. When, however, my affiliation with the Republicans became known, I paid the usual penalty of one who becomes a radical.

Not one of the so-called Americans who had promised to support me either spoke or voted for me. John S. Carlile was the only one straightforward enough to give me the reasons for the change. When I came into the House the day after the Philadelphia convention, Carlile came up to me and, in a frank and friendly tone, said: "Bennet, I can't give you my vote, as I promised. I know you have the right of your contest. But it is published that you were in the Black Republican convention, and if I should vote for you now, I could not sustain myself in my district. As an anti-administration man, I could have supported you, but not as a Republican." As I lost my contest by only three votes, I think it is very evident that my affiliation with the then radical party of the country cost me my seat.[38] The House, however, voted me $2,400 for my expenses as a contestant.[39]

On the whole, I felt that my contest had been worthwhile, notwithstanding my defeat. Even at the time I realized, though in a vague way, that the nation was entering upon one of the crucial periods of its existence. We were at the dynamic beginning of great movements in political thought and action, a period of confusion out of which new policies were becoming outlines, a time of stress and suppressed excitement which forewarned the wise of the coming clash of arms between the North and the South. In one sense, one might say the war began virtually with that memorable contest for the speakership of the House of Representatives—the struggle that lasted from the first Monday in December 1855 and resulted, as I have told, on the third of February 1856 in the election of Banks by the Republicans.

The great and dominant issue of the time was the question whether slave owners had the right to emigrate with their slaves into the new western territories. Besides the outright pro- and anti-slavery factions, there was a party of compromise led by Stephen A. Douglas. This party advocated "squatter sovereignty" or, as we would now term it, local option. It meant the right of the people of a territory to determine by their votes whether their territory should be admitted as a slave or a free state. The stress of the contention had become so great that Missouri, Kansas, and Nebraska were in a state of border warfare and Congress in an almost continuous struggle.

One day, chancing to step into the lobby of the Senate, I heard the closing remarks of John P. Hale, senator from New Hampshire, on some ordinary matter before the body. Some days previous, Hale had made a very able speech against slavery. It had greatly aroused the southern senators, particularly Clement C. Clay of Alabama, who next day in a bitter speech answered Hale. Clay was in wretched health, and his attempt to answer Hale's argument was as feeble as himself and remarkable only in its bitterness against Hale.

At this time Hale was not speaking on the slavery question but, as I have said, on some formal matter. As he concluded, he bent to sit down, then stood up again, and in the manner of a casual afterthought alluded to Clay's speech in a good-natured drawl: "Oh, I will only say further that no vituperation whatever will relieve imbecility from contempt." With that he dropped back into his seat. Clay looked daggers at him, and many of the senators were much concerned. But Hale sat cool and quiet, as though nothing unusual had been said. It was during this session that Preston S. Brooks, a representative in Congress from South Carolina, assaulted Charles Sumner of Massachusetts. The latter's seat in the Senate chamber was only a few feet distant from Hale's. There seems to be no doubt that Brooks intended to kill his victim, and he nearly succeeded in so doing. I was not in the Senate at the time, but on hearing of the assault I ran over from the House immediately after it happened.

Mr. Sumner was a large man, fully six feet tall. At the time of the attack he was sitting at his desk directing documents. His legs were extended under his desk and his face was close to his pen and paper, as he was quite nearsighted. While he was in this position, Brooks came up the narrow aisle in front of him.

Sumner did not see Brooks until the latter accosted him with threats and an uplifted cane. In attempting to rise, Sumner was first required to push his chair back, so that he might draw his legs from under the desk. In doing this, he leaned forward over the desk, with his head bent down quite low. At that moment, Brooks struck him a powerful blow with the uplifted cane, full on the back of his head. It was a heavy ebony cane; yet so violent was the blow, it was broken into many pieces, one of which I picked up from the floor when I reached the scene. Sumner, stunned by the blow, pitched forward, tearing loose his desk from its fastenings and also overturning the adjoining desk.

The best speech I heard during the entire session was one denouncing this dastardly assault. It was made by Anson Burlingame, a member of the House from Massachusetts. It took him an hour to deliver. His arraignment was as unanswerable by Brooks as Sumner's great speech against chattel slavery had been unanswerable by Senator Butler, Brooks's uncle. It was the attempt and failure of the latter that prompted the assault on Sumner.

Unable to match Burlingame in debate, Brooks challenged him to mortal combat—in other words, to fight a duel. Greatly to the surprise of the southerner, the challenge was promptly accepted by the dapper-looking little orator from Massachusetts. Burlingame proposed rifles at a distance of eighty yards, the place of meeting to be Canada, opposite Detroit. At this, Brooks made inquiries about the northerner and soon learned that he "had waked up the wrong man." Burlingame had been reared in Michigan and was a dead shot with a rifle. He was only too willing to accommodate southern chivalry with a trial by battle. The fight never occurred. I heard W. R. Cobb of Alabama, a southern member of the House, say at the time that Brooks backed down because he feared Burlingame's rifle.

A few weeks before the attack on Sumner, Horace Greeley was assaulted on the walk between the steps at the west side of the Capitol and Pennsylvania Avenue.[40] I was coming down the steps at the time and might have witnessed the occurrence had I been looking ahead, not down to where I was stepping. When I reached the bottom of the steps, I raised my eyes. About a hundred yards ahead of me I saw Mr. Burlingame adjusting Mr. Greeley's hat on his head. A few yards beyond them, General Rust and another member of the House were walking away. As far as my boardinghouse I walked down the avenue just behind Mr. Greeley. Rust and his companion were some distance ahead. Greeley stopped at the National Hotel and Rust went into Brown's.

This was a most brutal and cowardly assault on the part of Rust. It was unprovoked by any personal offense against him given by Greeley. The latter was in Washington much of the time during that session as the editorial correspondent of his paper, the *New York Tribune.* In every issue of his paper he criticized very severely the course of the slaveholders of the South in their efforts to carry their slave property into Kansas.

Rust was a man of about forty, a six-footer, massive and muscular. Greeley was older and, although of good size, looked anything else than a man of even ordinary physical force. He had a stooping form and shambling gait and looked far from strong. Besides all this disparity between the two men, Rust approached him and without warning struck him over the head and shoulders with a heavy hickory cane. This did not occur in the Capitol building nor was the assaulted party a member of Congress, as in the Sumner case.

There was some talk among the members of a resolution of censure against Rust, but nothing came of it. It was otherwise in the case of Brooks's assault on Sumner. A resolution for the expulsion of Brooks was introduced in the House by Louis Campbell, a member from Ohio. After several days of consideration and acrimonious debate by members of the House, the measure was passed by a small majority. So Preston S. Brooks was expelled from his seat in the House of Representatives.[41]

As soon as the vote was announced, Brooks left his seat and went into the gallery. When he sat down among the spectators, he was lustily cheered by a few members, friends of his in the House. He went home to South Carolina, was reelected, and returned to the same Congress. He died before the Civil War. I was told he ever regretted his assault on Sumner to the day of his death.[42] My own observation of him convinced me that he was very much of a gentleman, notwithstanding that attack on Sumner. No doubt he was enraged beyond control by the failure of his Senator uncle, Judge Butler, to refute Sumner's antislavery speech.

CHAPTER EIGHT

Adventures and Escapes 1856-1858

U PON LOSING MY CONTEST against Chapman, I at once left for home with my wife and child. We traveled by rail to Mount Pleasant, Iowa. There I bought a wagon and a two-horse team, and we continued our journey to Nebraska by wagon road, reaching home about the middle of August 1856. With me I brought a pocketful of money, to say nothing of the valuable education in politics that I had acquired during my stay of eight months in Washington. Instead of being discouraged, I had become all the more ambitious for a political career.

During that summer a party of surveyors [arrived] for the survey of the public lands between Salt Creek and the Weeping Water, Nebraska. After my return home, one of Colonel Menners's chairmen, late in the afternoon of a bright August day, came wild-eyed into Nebraska. He was weary and haggard, having, he said, fled for his life from Indians who had attacked the surveying party between the headwaters of Salt Creek and Weeping Water, some fifty miles away. He told that the Indians had killed all others of the surveyors and he alone had escaped to tell the tale. This information greatly excited the town, for it was here that the surveying party had been made up and most members of it were well-known young men. A public meeting promptly resolved on steps to organize a force to go to the scene of the massacre with the purpose of rescuing any of the party yet living, if any, and to bring in the bodies of the dead.

The plan of campaign was soon arranged. Twelve scouts, mounted on the fleetest horses in town, were to leave that night at twelve o'clock. By a rapid march they should before daylight reach the ford on Weeping Water two or three miles the near side of the trouble. There they were to go into hiding in the bushes along the stream and as best they could spy out the enemy. The main force was to follow in the morning, fully equipped with supplies, and reach the Weeping Water sometime that night. Twelve men volunteered as scouts, all saying they had good horses. I was one of them, and, as it afterwards proved, had the best mount of all. We agreed to meet at the courthouse at twelve midnight sharp. But on the hour appointed only six of the twelve appeared. Having no time to lose, we six did not wait a minute for the laggards but left at once.

It was a lively ride that tried well the wind and mettle of our horses. The excitement of the occasion made us quite regardless of fatigue and loss of sleep. But apprehension of danger from the Indians sobered us when, a little after sunrise, we came in sight of the valley of the Weeping Water and of the ford a mile off. Though low trees and willows along the banks covered the view, we expected to see at least some signs of the enemy. Casting our eyes down just ahead of us in the trail, we saw fresh tracks of ponies going towards the ford. That hushed our loud talk and rallying of each other, which up to that time we had been doing to keep up our courage.

With pistols in hands and hearts in our throats, we slowly and quietly approached the ford in double file. I was one of the middle pair. Two were in front and two in the rear. In that order and line of battle we moved down a long slope to the ford. After coming within gunshot of the brush, we expected every moment a volley from the lurking foe. We thought they were lying in ambush to await our coming. Ready for battle, we passed through the thickets and down the steep bank of the stream, which was only a few yards wide at the ford. At sight of the water, our thirsty horses crowded together in the stream, eager to quench their thirst after the forty-mile run over a dry and dusty road. It is a well-known fact that a thirsty horse, when ridden into a running stream, will invariably turn upstream as he plunges his nose into the water. This, I suppose, is the more readily to receive the water into his parched mouth and throat.

Still on the alert and still, as I thought, in the midst of the enemy seeking me for a mark of his deadly aim, I heard a slight noise behind me. When I quickly turned in the saddle and looked to see the cause, I at once saw, to my surprise and relief, not a band of bloodthirsty savages, ready to take our scalps, but *two mules!* The pair were harnessed together with the lines and tugs dragging and their heads checked up. They stood in the water seeking to get at the grass that grew on the steep banks. Sight of the homely animals gave me instant relief from my dread of Indians about to shoot and scalp me.

I broke the long silence of our party by a loud *whoop!* It greatly startled my comrades. But all were reassured when they saw the cause of my shout and realized we were in no danger. Our first proceeding was to get the half-starved mules out of the stream and unchecked so that they could graze. With them following, we went into camp across the ford, under the shade of some cottonwood trees, a short distance down the far bank. There we unsaddled our horses and turned them out with the mules to graze on the rich grass. After enjoying the lunch we had brought along, we stretched out to take a nap in the cool of the morning. I had picketed my horse near where I lay with my saddle for [a] pillow. The other animals were all loose.

About two hours after we went to sleep, I was wakened by the tramping of a band of animals. The lariat of my horse was drawn taut across my body and held me down. My first thought was that the Indians were upon us. But on struggling up to look, I saw no attackers. Instead, the two mules and every horse of our party except my own were on the run towards the ford. After immediately arousing my comrades, I saddled my horse and started in pursuit of the others. But so rapid was their flight for home that I failed to overtake them. Having pursued them for some four miles, I gave up the chase and returned to the camp.

If Indians had been the cause of our misfortune, they would have run the animals in a different direction. We all came to the conclusion that it must have been the heat and flies that had stampeded the stock, for both bothered us greatly after we were left afoot. With no horse except my own, we could not go further towards the scene of the massacre of the surveyors. All we could do was to await the arrival of the main party, which we expected to reach us sometime that night. When the sun was getting low in the afternoon, its horizontal rays licked up all shade under the large cottonwood trees. We moved camp to the ford, into the shade of a clump of willows. There we rested in peace and quiet, excepting always for mosquitoes, which caused us no little loss of blood.

The main "army" had started in due season that morning, fully equipped with arms and commissary stores. It also had a full supply of medicine, especially that kind called "snake medicine," very much used by civilians in the cure of snakebite. This was wisely provided for the campaign by our surgeon general, who had long used such medicine in his practice. So the army had come on apace, in great spirits, eager to kill every Indian of the Oto tribe. When some twenty miles on their march, lo and behold! they saw coming in the distance a band in a cloud of dust. This looked to our gallant fighters like a party of Indians. A line of battle was at once formed, and the approaching band was captured. It proved to be the horses and mules that had left us so unceremoniously in the morning. This greatly excited the troops and hurried their march. They felt sure the Indians had attacked us scouts in camp and that the noise of firing had stampeded the stock before the savages got through killing and scalping us.

The fast advance brought the party to the hill overlooking the valley where we were camped behind the clump of willows. Seeing them before they saw us, we started a little willow fire to raise a smoke. Then with our saddle blankets about us, Indianlike, we dodged in and out of the willows. When the warrior host came near enough to see these maneuvers, they halted, got out their arms, and advanced cautiously. They came within gunshot and again halted. Judging that they were about to open fire on us, we all ran into full view and cast off our blankets. Thus suddenly undeceived, the party were so relieved and rejoiced that they plied whips and spurs and came rushing down upon us in the wildest confusion.

All camped there that night. But few if any were able to sleep owing to the swarms of ferocious mosquitoes. To offset the poison of their bites, we consumed all our store of "snake medicine."

Next day, after being joined by reinforcements from Plattsmouth, we proceeded to the Indian village near the mouth of Salt Creek. There we met some of the chiefs. They told us that their people had not injured a single man of the surveying party nor touched an article of their property. They explained that a war party returning from the plains saw the surveyors a few miles from the village. Thinking to "show off big" before this party of white men, they had charged at them in true Indian style, yelling and whooping as in battle. This was all in playful imitation of war and not with any intention whatever of scaring or hurting the white men.

The surveyors, however, had never had much to do with Indians. Seeing the war party coming at them in such menacing manner, they unhitched their teams, dropped everything, and ran for their lives. The man with the compass left it standing on the line; the chainmen dropped the chain. Some ways off, the man driving their camp wagon saw the Indians charging down upon the others. He hastily unhitched his mules from the wagon and mounted one of the wheel team. He fled, trusting that the other mules would follow. One of them did keep him company all the thirty miles or so to Plattsmouth. The lead team we found in the Weeping Water, as I have told. After that pretended attack, the Indians had retired to their village and the remaining surveyors had resumed their work. When certain of this last, our "army" marched home from the campaign without having lost a single man.

Later in 1857 I was present at a payment of annuity to the Sac and Fox Indians on their reservation in northeastern Kansas. The payment was made in silver money and in goods consisting of Mackinaw blankets, red, white, blue, and green; bright-colored cloths for the squaws; and a large quantity of flour, rice, salt, sugar, and coffee; also beads and other trinkets. Most interesting of all to the Indians was a big herd of beef cattle. These animals the bucks slaughtered in sight of the treaty camp. They turned them loose on the open prairie in imitation of a buffalo hunt, chasing and killing them from horseback. Never before or since did I hear such yelling and whooping. The squaws and papooses joined in the chorus while following the chase to butcher the beeves as they fell. Not a scrap of the animals was wasted by the Indians. They threw away no more of the carcasses than a Chicago packer does of his pigs.

Much of the annuity money went to pay the trader. He had supplied the tribe since their last payment with ammunition and other necessities—and, like as not, with whiskey *sub rosa*. With what was left of their money the men proceeded to spend the afternoon and evening in gambling. In this the squaws were not permitted to share. Four or five young bucks would spread a blanket on the ground. Seated around its edges, they would play at a game not unlike "Button, button, who has the button?" A small shawl or piece of cloth was spread out on the blanket, and the one who had the lead would put, or pretend to put, the "button" under the cloth, with or without his ante, as he chose.

It was then up to the others to guess what he had done, each guess requiring a bet. If one of them guessed right, he took the pot, with the ante, if any, and whatever had been agreed upon as the value of the button. If nothing was found under the cloth when the guesses, or bets, were all in, the first player took the pot. During the game the players kept time with a rattle to a series of short guttural grunts uttered in a rhythmical monotone. This, I suppose, was considered to be singing, and it was not unpleasant even to our ears.

During 1857 Harry Blackman had come into the law firm of which I was a member. Shortly afterwards I drew out of the partnership. That

August I was elected to the legislature of Nebraska. There was a call for a special session, and of this I was made Speaker of the House. The special session lasted until the time for the beginning of the regular one, and I was continued on as Speaker until the close of the latter session. At the time I was a Republican. Not an Abolitionist, as were some. I still favored the right to hold Negroes as slaves *in the southern states.* Contradictory as it seems, I was opposed to the extension of slavery or the holding of slaves in territor[ies] not yet admitted as states, although, at the same time, I believed in "squatter sovereignty." This last meant that when a new state was to be admitted, the inhabitants should have the right to decide by vote whether theirs should be a free or a slave state. These were very controversial issues. At the time of the passing from the special to the regular session of the legislature, nearly all the members of the House celebrated the occasion until they were very "mellow" but also hot-tempered. While in committee they became so wrought up that the occasion might have ended in a bloody fight. Governor Richardson rushed in among the struggling members crying, "Peace! peace! Damn you, peace!" That put an end to the disgraceful scene.

Owing to the financial crisis of 1857, a great many "wildcat" banks all over the country failed. John H. Maxon and myself were sent by the Platte Valley Bank of Nebraska City to make a run on the banks of Council Bluffs. This was to be in retaliation for a run made by them on our bank the morning of the day we started.[43] As ammunition for our attack we were provided with some $13,000 in the bills of the Council Bluffs banks.

About 2:00 P.M. we set off from Nebraska City in my buggy, driving a span of horses of which I had reason to be proud. One was a grey and other a black, and both were good travelers. The distance to be covered was fifty miles, and our way was by the river road, which was in good condition. We carried no firearms and no baggage other than the money. Riding thus in a light buggy behind a spirited team, we sped along our way. Our only thought was of the gratification it would give us to get even with the Council Bluffs banks for the fun they had made on the one represented by us.

Night overtook us when we had covered about half of our journey. But we kept on, without any thought of danger, driving by the light of the moon, which was playing hide-and-seek with the clouds. A mile or two beyond the town of St. Mary's, we passed through a strip of timber. As we emerged on the farther side, the moon shone out brightly and we caught sight of three men, two or three hundred yards distant, coming towards us along the road. Neither my companion nor myself spoke. But I, for one, was very much concerned. As I have stated, we were unarmed, and if these men proved to be robbers our only chance to escape lay in the speed of my horses.

Gripping the reins firmly in one hand, and with the whip in the other, I kept my team right along at their ordinary gait as though the men had not been within a mile of us and my heart not in my mouth for fear they might be "holdups." We were within a few feet of them when one stepped into the middle of the road. The other two came forward a little, one on each side of the road, forming a triangle. As I drove into this, all three of the fellows were within a few feet of us. The horses were slackening their gait when the man on our left called out, "Halt!" Instantly I gave my horses a quick cut with my whip, which I had been holding in readiness to do this, or to strike the face and eyes of the holdup on my right. At the sharp slash, the horses sprang forward so quickly that the fellow in front of them barely escaped being run down.

Away we flew, the horses doing their best and my companion and myself crouched down over the dashboard. At every moment we expected a volley of pistol bullets. Even when we found ourselves safe beyond gunshot, I did not slacken speed. I kept the horses at the same rapid pace until, about two miles farther on, we reached a house. Here we stopped for a few minutes to breathe the horses and try to get some firearms. But all about the house was dark and silent, and there being no indication that we were pursued, we went on again without rousing the sleeping family. The horses held to a moderately sharp pace. It brought us to Council Bluffs about one o'clock in the morning with no further trouble other than our fear of about every dark object standing near the road.

The reason why the highwaymen did not fire on us was, I believe, owing to the fact that the men who that morning had made the run on the Platte Valley Bank drove a team of sorrel horses. In all likelihood the robbers had learned of that intended run and lain in wait to capture the proceeds from the agents of the Council Bluffs bankers on their way home. When we came up close, the color of my horses must have caused them to doubt that we were the party for whom they were waiting. Then they saw our faces and knew we were not the Council Bluffs men. They evidently became confused and uncertain just what to do. But the fellow who was to cry "Halt!" let the word go at a venture. Had we obeyed the command, they would have stolen twice as much money as they could have got from the Council Bluffs party. As it was, being confused and uncertain, they concluded not to fire, or at any rate they hesitated to do so until we were well beyond their reach.

The next day we made a successful haul out of the Council Bluffs banks. Then, after providing ourselves with firearms, we returned home by the way we had come. But this time we traveled in broad daylight, arriving safely that evening.

During the following year, 1858, tension between the proslavery and antislavery factions became extremely hot and bitter. One day at Nebraska City a mob gathered in front of the office of Surveyor General Callwen, who was proslavery. They threatened to do violence to Callwen and to several of his employees. William H. Taylor, a lawyer, stood up in a lumber wagon and fierily addressed the mob, urging them to "clean out" the whole office of the surveyor general. The infuriated Free Soilers were on the point of making the attack when I climbed up beside Taylor. I whispered in his ear to let me make a single remark. Knowing that I was politically hostile to Callwen, he at once paused in his tirade.

At that I burst out in a tirade of my own. With a few impassioned words I turned the purpose of the crowd to the pursuit of a ruffian who had fired a pistol at one of our friends and, as we thought, had mortally wounded him. Within another five minutes, had I not stopped Taylor's harangue, there would have been shots fired and the mob in full rage. As it was, all danger of violence was at an end by the time I had finished my interruption. Most of the angry men scattered in all directions, intent upon the capture of the escaped desperado.

The attack upon the office of the surveyor general was never made. Even Taylor had cooled down. When I surrendered the "floor" to him, though he looked baffled, he was not angry with me over the way I had tricked him.

CHAPTER NINE

Pikes Peak Days   1859-1860

IN THE EARLY PART of 1859, I failed to obtain the nomination of the Republican convention of Nebraska for delegate to Congress. There were other reasons to make me restless. I had suffered no little from sickness for the past two years and more, and had lost my third and only surviving child. Moreover, there was little to be gained by the practice of my profession at Nebraska City. All lines of business were dull, not having recovered from the financial crisis of 1857, when all our western "wildcat" banks went broke. As the government was not behind the banks, all who held the bills of these private state banks, as well as the depositors, lost their money. Also, in the midst of my depression, my youngest brother, William, had come home from a two-months' trip as a government surveyor out on the prairie some two hundred miles west of Nebraska City. He had suffered greatly from heat, thirst, and exposure and was so much reduced in health and strength that I scarcely knew him. The doctors said he had developed pulmonary consumption from an attack of pneumonia two years previous. They advised a change of climate.

Owing to all these conditions I decided to move out to the Pikes Peak country. Aside from the prospects offered by the gold rush, I understood that the climate there would be the best for my brother. This was in August 1859. I sold William's place and my own in Nebraska City, both at a sacrifice. With the proceeds I bought us an outfit that included two ox teams, two wagons, two horses, and two cows. We started for the mountains the latter part of September accompanied by our wives.

Leonard Silvernail, a consumptive boy from Massachusetts, and Ramon Guiteriez, a young Spanish American, took turns driving my brother's wagon. My wife and I also took turns driving our own. The horses were led behind my wagon, and the cows, after a few days' travel in the yoke, followed without need of tying.

George H. Vickroy and Thomas Barnum, who drove mule teams, traveled with us most of the way up the Platte. Fortunately few of the Plains Indians had gone on the warpath, for the four able-bodied men of our little wagon train had only shotguns, no rifles.[44] Even so, the trip was a hard one for us all. As wagon master, it had devolved upon me to ride ahead in the afternoon to select the night camp. At such times my wife, sitting in the front end of our covered "prairie schooner," drove the ox team with a long whip. It was well that all our oxen were gentle and well broken. I had bought them from a Mormon who had come to Nebraska City from Nauvoo only a few months before.

Making camp was the hardest of my work, above all my task of setting up the big twelve-foot-wall tent in which my brother, myself, and our wives slept. Silvernail and the other men slept in or under the wagons. My brother was too feeble to do anything, and as his wife also was not very strong, most of the cooking fell to the share of my wife. The other men of the party had their hands full unhitching the teams, picketing out the mules and horses, and gathering fuel. The cooking was done over the campfire with frying pan and skillet and kettles for boiling potatoes, coffee, etc. For bread we had soda biscuits and flapjacks. This, with potatoes and salt pork, of which I had a great abundance, was our main diet. We seldom had fresh meat. Though we often sighted buffalo and antelope, we had, as I have told, no rifles, only shotguns, and none of us was a Nimrod.

One afternoon, while in camp at Plum Creek west of Fort Kearney, I went out with two of the boys on a still hunt over the bluffs to the south of the river. We found a small herd of buffalo in the hollows among the hills and managed to get near enough to have bagged some of the big fellows if we had had rifles. Several large, white wolves skulked about the herd waiting a chance to cut out a buffalo calf or to feast on what we left should we make a killing. They had more reason to be disappointed over our failure to bring down a buffalo than were we, for on our way back I managed to shoot a jack rabbit. When we reached camp we did our best to convince the women that the rabbit was a buffalo calf. They were too obstinate to believe us. However, the rabbit gave us a supper of fresh meat that was as good or better than buffalo hump, which is the best part of that animal.

Our night camps, pitched near the low, grassy banks of the Platte, were uniformly agreeable. The river water in those early days and at that time of year was clear, pure, and very sweet. In the morning the water that had stood in the pails overnight would be cool and as clear as crystal. With a little sugar and a jigger of gin added to it from a tap in Vickroy's uncovered wagon, it would give our herders courage to rush off before the sunup breakfast to find the stock. The animals often wandered far out of sight during the night in search of better grass. This "ginning up" was quite an event with the herders. I myself found it no disagreeable way to start the day when I turned out at daybreak to build the fire and start breakfast to cooking.

I could boil potatoes and fry bacon but had to leave the making of the biscuits to my wife. She baked them in a skillet. Afterwards I learned from Major Oakes and old Jim Baker to bake bread by winding strips of dough around a clean stick. The stick was then stuck up in the ground beside the campfire and the dough baked by turning the stick around as the cooking proceeded.

After thirty-five days of weary travel, we reached the abandoned old fort of St. Vrain, near Platteville, in the early part of October. There Vickroy and Barnum parted company with us, going to the Arkansas River. We remained in camp at the fort for a two-weeks' rest.

Continuing on along the Platte, we reached the mouth of Clear Creek, then still known as Vasquez Fork. Driving up the creek, we came to the ford of the Cherokee Trail, at what is now North Tennyson Street a quarter mile outside the present boundary of Denver. This old trail came from the Arkansas River near Bent's Fort. Thence it ran westerly across the hills to the Fountain Boulle [Fountaine qui Bouille], within twenty miles of the later site of Pueblo. It then came up Squirrel Creek, over the Divide, down Cherry Creek, and across the site of Denver to the crossing of Clear Creek. Beyond the ford the trail held on its way north to La Porte on the Cache la Poudre, then west across the mountains at Cameron Pass, and continued far west to Bridger's Pass, Fort Bridger, Salt Lake, and so on to California.

To go back to Clear Creek. Sometime after our crossing of the Cherokee Trail, Jim Baker, the noted trapper and Indian scout, built a toll bridge at the ford.[45] He and his Shoshone wife lived in a cabin on the south bank. The graves of two of their daughters, up along the top of the bank, were still marked as late as 1910.

In 1859 there were comparatively few trees in the creek bottom. Journeying on upstream, we at last turned out of its valley to drive around the north end of North Table Mountain and down into Golden City. Here we thought, for a time, was the end of our travels. I bought lots and built two cabins, one for my own family and one for my brother and his wife. At that time Golden hoped to become the "metropolis" of the gold rush towns. But upon going down to the twin settlement of Auraria-Denver, I decided that there was the most promising location. Accordingly, on December 24, 1859, I rented a log cabin at the corner of Ferry and Larimer streets in Auraria (soon to become West Denver). Both of our families moved down there from Golden. My wife brought the first cow to Denver. She traded the animal for a cookstove. The house in Auraria remained our home for a year or more. But my brother William died January 12, 1860.

Upon moving down from Golden, I had at once "put up my shingle" as a lawyer [in] the office of a lumberyard owned by Maj. D. C. Oakes.[46] There I started practice under the several jurisdictions then covering the so-called territory of Jefferson—the Pikes Peak region. There was a full set of officers for the county of Arapahoe appointed by Governor Denver of Kansas; also a lot of officers, including a judge of the district court, for the territory of Jefferson. In the mountain towns were miners' courts for crimes such as murder and for arbitrating claim-jumping. A secret vigilante committee dealt with horse and cattle thieves, usually by hanging them.[47] Except for these entirely unlegal lynch law proceedings, I practiced in all kinds of trials. Defendants found guilty by the more regular courts were, according to the degree of their crimes, either given a heavy lashing or banished from the territory or hanged.

Early in March 1860 I had the unpleasant experience of being a spectator at two duels. The first one, which was between Louis Bliss and Dr. Stone, resulted in the death of the latter, who was the challenger. Shortly after this disgraceful tragedy Park McClure, Denver's first postmaster, sent a challenge to Ed Wynkoop, the city marshal of Denver under the People's government. The challenge was accepted and the parties met for the duel. But on the ground, McClure changed his mind about fighting. After a fruitless effort to have Wynkoop withdraw the offensive words that had been the cause of the challenge, he back[ed] down and the affair ended in a fiasco.[48] This was very well for McClure, as he probably surmised. In all probability he would have met the same fate as Dr. Stone. It was certainly a more sensible and civilized way to end the matter than for the two men to have stood up to the scratch and tried to murder each other.

A few days after the Stone-Bliss duel there had occurred a tragedy of a somewhat different nature. Moses Young, a carpenter and builder, and a man named William West had come out from Leavenworth, Kansas, where they had worked together. They took cabins a few rods apart on Cherry Street in Denver and continued to work together. Then some difference arose between them. One day when Young was at West's cabin, they talked the matter over, apparently without heat or passion on either side. Young then returned to his own cabin. Shortly afterwards, West left home and started along the street. He was in the middle of it, opposite Young's cabin, when Young came to his door with a double-barreled shotgun in his hands, and called out: "I've got you now!" With that, he fired. West sank down and died without a word, having been struck by seventeen buckshot.

At the time I was in a house on the east bank of Cherry Creek trying a case before Justice of the Peace Wyatt. All of us in the courtroom were startled by the sound of the shot and ran out in the street to learn what it meant. We saw several men running towards a point in Cherry Street that was shut off from our view by a large log cabin. I started at once to cross the Larimer Street bridge. On it I passed Young walking very rapidly in the opposite direction, going, I supposed, for a doctor. A few moments afterwards I reached the spot where West was lying in his blood. Someone remarked that he had been shot by Young. At this I told about meeting Young. The crowd at once started in pursuit of him. I returned to finish the trial of my case, then started for home.

In the meantime the whole town had learned of the killing, and nearly everybody was out looking for the murderer, greatly excited. My home, as I have told, was on the west side near where the Davis Flour Mill was afterwards built. I was sitting with my wife when, about sundown, we heard a great shouting and yelling over on Blake Street near Fifteenth. At once I started out to learn the cause of the noise. Recrossing the bridge where earlier in the day I had met Young, I hurried on, urged forward by the howling and yelling of a great mob. When I reached the corner of Fifteenth and Larimer, I caught sight of the leaders of the mob just coming around the corner of Sixteenth with Young.

Jim O'Neill, a "gentleman ruff," to use the term then in vogue, had found the murderer secreted under a lot of harness and tackle in a loft over the saloon of "Ki" Harrison. He had no doubt been hidden there by the saloonkeeper. Jim brought him out at the point of a Navy revolver and delivered him over to the crowd. It was at this time the shouting began that I heard at my home across the creek. When I arrived the mob was terribly excited, nearly everyone in it yelling, "Hang him! Hang him!"

As they came surging forward, I jumped upon a dry goods box that happened to be standing beside the little building at the corner of Fifteenth Street. I began to yell at the top of my voice, "Hang him, the bloody murderer! Hang him!" This gave the crowd the idea not only that I was with them but that I was even more vehement in advocating the lynching of their victim. My position on the box gave me an advantage, and I shouted so energetically that when the mob came up before me they halted and fell silent to hear what I had to say. By this means I "got the floor" and at once went on as loudly and in as excited a manner as possible. I shouted that we must not let the red-handed murderer escape; that we must hang him, not in any halfway, bungling manner but without making any mistake about it—in a decent and becoming manner.

Seeing a tall, resolute man whom I knew standing near the prisoner, armed with a big Navy revolver, I called upon him to at once organize a guard of fifty men, armed with double-barreled shotguns, to guard the prisoner and make certain that he did not escape. The organization of the guard was immediately begun. It was rapidly carried on while I continued to hold the crowds by extravagant denunciations of the prisoner. By the time several of the guard had been collected about Young, the mob had begun to lose some of its heat. At the same time I began to tone down my voice and manner.

Still maintaining the floor, I went on to say that we were all law-abiding and peaceful men; that there was none of us who would willingly do a man a wrong, and that everyone of us was in favor of fair play. We should and would hang this murderer of poor old William West. But, as they saw, he was now safely guarded, and so, as a matter of fair play, we should first give him a chance to be heard in his own defense before we hang him.

By this time it was sundown, which prompted me to suggest that the prisoner be held by the guard until the next morning. We could then organize a People's Court with a jury made up of our best-known citizens and thereby try, convict, and hang the murderer in an orderly and decent manner. We owed it even more to ourselves than to the prisoner to wait until, boldly and aboveboard, in the broad light of day, we could give the prisoner a fair trial. Seeing that we were without statute or other law than the laws of God and nature, we should do this in the most proper, legal, and orderly manner possible.

Then, before surrendering the floor, I put the question to the crowd. Without a dissenting voice, the motion was carried to wait and give the prisoner a fair trial the next day. Bright and early the next morning, the crowd assembled in the Elephant Corral building on Blake Street. A paper had been drawn up and signed by many requesting Judge Wyatt, James Gray, and myself to act as prosecuting attorneys. Before the court was organized, Wyatt and Gray backed out and declined to prosecute. This left me the sole prosecuting attorney in the case. The defendant was represented by attorneys A. C. Ford, Jim Coleman, Ham Hunt, and three others.

There were present fully a thousand people. It was in fact an open town meeting. Three judges and twenty-four jurymen, all from among the best known citizens, were named and elected by a vote of the meeting. A. C. Hunt, elected as presiding judge, swore in with due formality and solemnity his fellow judges and the twenty-four jurors, and the trial then began. Witnesses both for the prosecution and the defense were sworn and gave their testimony. The fullest opportunity was given the prisoner to present any defense that he might have; but he could show none. On the other hand, it was shown by the prosecution that the killing was due to the fact that West would not agree to cancel the mortgage on a lot in Leavenworth belonging to Young until the mortgage indebtedness had been paid.

The trial lasted all day. Then the jury withdrew apart. It at once unanimously agreed on a verdict of guilty of murder in the first degree. When Hunt had announced the verdict, he submitted it to a vote of the assembly, which had remained present throughout the trial, and the verdict was endorsed without a dissenting vote. The prisoner was then told to stand up, and, in due form, he was sentenced by Judge Hunt to be hung the next day between the hours of eleven and twelve.

A scaffold was erected in Cherry Street between Larimer and Market over the spot where West had fallen and where his life's blood yet discolored the ground. Upon that scaffold, promptly within the hour named, Moses Young was hung for the willful and unprovoked murder of William West. On Tuesday, March 12, 1860, the murder was committed; on Wednesday the thirteenth the murderer was tried for the crime; on Thursday the fourteenth he was hung.[49]

At the time of this occurrence, all the country that is now known as Colorado was without legally established law, whether federal, state, or territorial. It is true that nominally Denver was then in what was known as the county of Arapahoe of the territory of Kansas. But when, a short time before, Kansas had been admitted as a state, its western boundary had been established along the east line of Arapahoe

County. Between this time and the organization of the territory of Colorado in 1861, the large population from the eastern states who had rushed into the country during the Pikes Peak gold excitement found themselves living in a "no man's land." Deprived of all law and authority from without, the people fell back on the right of self-defense and established their own laws and tribunals.

Though I received no fee for my prosecution of Young, the part I took in the affair was like "bread cast upon the waters." It and other prosecutions of murderers made me so well known that when Colorado was organized as a territory by Congress, I was nominated and elected as the first delegate to Congress from Colorado, and in 1862 was reelected for a second term. Before this, aided by A. C. Hunt and Andrew Sagendorf, I had started a movement for a regular People's Court.[50] At a public meeting the plans for such a court were adopted. Maj. Jacob Downing and Niles Sargeant were selected by acclamation as judges. This court followed the Iowa statutes, since they were the only ones in town. They were taken from my law library. Being by far the largest and most valuable collection—fourteen volumes—they caused me to be regarded as the legal oracle of the country.[51] I was chosen public prosecutor.

In spite of the strenuous efforts of others and myself, the self-appointed vigilantes continually took the law in their own hands. It was not an uncommon sight to see one to six human bodies hanging from posts in an early morning. With the cooperation of Major Downing, I had at once commenced a vigorous campaign to drive out all desperadoes. Within a period of thirty days I prosecuted, and Downing sentenced, 125 men. During my term, I can say that, in spite of threats, I never hesitated to prosecute or speak out against the bad men, though I always went unarmed.

Aiding Downing and myself in our campaign for law and order, the *Rocky Mountain News* in every issue battled the lawless element. Carl Woods, the leader of the desperadoes, threatened to destroy the *News.* While threats were being passed back and forth, Charles Harrison killed a Negro named Starks. Although he claimed the killing was in self-defense, the *News* condemned the incident in bitter language. Woods and his gang captured William Byers, editor of the *News*, and took him to the Criterion Saloon to apologize to Harrison. As a preliminary to the apology, Woods ordered drinks for the crowd. While the liquor was being served, Harrison let Byers out the back door. When Byers got back to the *News* office, he armed all of his employees and barred the doors. Within a few minutes, Woods and his gang were outside the building, blazing away with their guns. It was quickly rumored through the town that Byers had been killed. A large posse was organized, and Woods was captured and held for trial. Since Byers was very much alive, Woods could not be tried for murder. Charges of lawlessness and disturbing the peace were preferred against the desperado. I was selected as judge of the extemporaneous court and presided over the three-day trial. The sentence of the court that Woods should be banished forever from the territory was carried out immediately at the end of the trial.

One of the important trials in the People's Court was that of James Gordon for murder. Gordon, who had conducted a number of atrocious murders, was captured and returned to Denver by W. H. Middaugh, who secured a special appointment as United States deputy marshal for this purpose. The trial was held under a cottonwood tree at the corner of Fifteenth and Wazee streets. A. C. Hunt was the presiding judge; H. R. Hunt, W. P. McClure, and J. H. Sherman were appointed as counsel for Gordon. Besides myself, Jacob Downing and James Coleman presented the people's case. The trial lasted from September 18 to October 2. When the issue was submitted, the people unanimously voted guilty. On the sixth of October, Gordon was hanged on a scaffold located on the site where the Evans home was later built. The last case heard in the People's Court occurred November 30, 1850 [1860], when Pat Waters was tried for murder. I prosecuted this case and secured a verdict of guilty. Waters was hanged December 20.[52]

A young lawyer, Moses Hallett, who many years later became a federal court judge, had come out in 1859 to prospect for gold. Not making a strike, he planned to return East. Instead, I took him into my office as a law clerk and soon made him my partner.[53] In 1864, while I was in Congress, the great Cherry Creek flood swept away our office building, along with hundreds of others.[54] Later on, riding down the Platte, Hallett came upon a chicken coop with the sign "Bennet and Hallett, Attorneys at Law."

Mr. Lincoln was elected president after a very bitter canvass on the question of the extension of slavery to the territories of the United States. This bitter feeling continued with increasing intensity all over the country, especially throughout the southern or slave states. It resulted in the secession of several of them before the fourth of March, 1861. The people of all the states soon divided into two parties, union and disunion. There were many southerners in Denver who were blatant rebels or secessionists. They secretly organized and drilled a military company and picked up all the firearms to be found in town.

Wallingford and Murphy, who occupied a large log building with goods and merchandise, raised a rebel flag atop their store one day the latter part of January 1861. This aroused the feeling of Union men as no mere "sechesh" talk would do. The rebel flag had not been up long before some fifteen or twenty of us Union men got together on the corner of Fifteenth and Larimer in sight of the flag. It was a cheap, dirty white cloth with a dark figure of some kind in the middle. We were not near enough to make out just what it was, but took it for a snake coiled, ready to strike. We did not stand there long to consider what to do. We quickly sent a committee to tell Wallingford and Murphy to take down that sechesh flag at once, else we would come and do it for them. The committee delivered their message and returned, and soon we saw the flag disappear, never to be seen again in Denver.

This brief little affair, however, did not put a stop to rebel talk. It continued on the streets, in front of saloons and gambling places. The impending rebellion was the subject of discussions, mostly by the southern sympathizers, no matter who was present. But few disputes over the conditions of the country took place. For the Union men deprecated all hostile expression and declared always for peace here and unity among themselves to make common defense against the Indians, who might fight to drive us all out of the country. For this reason we got along without any actual hostilities during the winter.

Yet like several of my friends and associates, I could not get over the insult of that rebel flag. Notwithstanding that we had come off victorious over the affair, we yet were in grave doubt of having a majority of Unionists who would take part in a like case, should another occur. Having stood this uncertainty as long as I could, I determined that a counter demonstration should be made to find out how many people in Denver were on our side. As Washington's Birthday was only a short way off, I thought it would be a fitting time to fly our "Star Spangled Banner" to the breeze.[55]

Without consulting with anyone about my purpose, I inquired around town for a U. S. flag. There was none to be had. But I had seen one on the stone house of the Boston Company at Golden. I purchased it from them by trading in a Golden lot, nominally worth twenty-five dollars. Bringing the precious bunting home to Denver, I stored it under my pillow in the care of my wife. Next I sent to Tucker's Gulch, in the mountains above Golden, for the longest pole the boys could find that was not too large to be handled on the wagon. They returned with one about thirty feet long, barked and dry and light to handle. On the twenty-first I went over town to get a halyard with which to raise the flag. As I could find no small line, I had to take a three-quarter-inch lariat for the purpose. Up to this time, no one except my wife knew what I was up to.

That same evening I ordered some liquid refreshments sent over to my house for the next morning. This was not for myself but for others, some of whom I thought might be wavering or hesitating over their loyalty. After a good drink of whiskey, I hoped that the sight of the old flag on a liberty pole would cause them to join the shout for the Union. Old Glory and three gallons of good liquor ought to be enough to win over every man present on the occasion. As further inspiration, I had engaged a brass band—the only one, I think, in town—to come at 2 P.M. and play quickstep music.

My home on the west side was a mansion of one room, twelve by fourteen, with a lean-to for a kitchen. East and south of it was prairie, and the pole was to be set up about fifty feet away from the house, on the open ground. The evening before, I got word all over town that there would be a flag-raising at my home at two o'clock on Washington's Birthday. Everybody was to come and have a good time.

On the morning of the twenty-second I had a sick headache. But with some help I managed to get the hole dug for the pole, and the pulley and halyard properly attached in readiness for the great ceremony to come. The band came about half past two, playing a lively tune. Behind followed a quiet crowd of perhaps 150 persons. Without hesitation they helped set the pole up in place. Grasping the halyard, I called upon the band to play "The Star Spangled Banner." Up went the flag to the top of the pole; caught by the breeze, it spread out and triumphantly waved overhead.

Thrilled at the sight, all members of the crowd burst into applause. Some sang the words of the grand old patriotic anthem, others hurrahed. Wildly excited, they hugged and slapped each other and jumped into the air as they looked up at the flag. There were tears of joy in some eyes, and my own were moist. And so it continued until the band ceased playing. Had I known beforehand that a sight of the old flag afloat in Denver would have inspired such an outburst of patriotic feeling, I could have left out the liquid refreshments. But the whiskey was on the ground, and though not needed to enthuse the crowd, it was passed around; needless to say, it added to the pleasure of the occasion.

Soon the speaking began. Though first called on, I declined because of my now violent headache. To take my place I called upon one DeMar, a young lawyer, whom I knew to be a little shaky on the Union question. He at once responded with a few words of love for the old flag. In concluding his speech, he asked me why in hell I had got too big a rope for a halyard. The flag, he said, was light and easy to pull up; the smallest boy in the crowd was strong enough to have done it, and, like all "young America," would have been glad of the chance. In answer, instead of telling it was the smallest line I had been able to find for the purpose, I repeated what General Dix had said a few weeks before about pulling down the U. S. flag. The rope, I explained, had to be big and strong enough to pull up by the neck any rebel who dared to pull down our country's flag. That brought a great shout of approval.

The whiskey continued to be passed around until all the three gallons were gone. I sent for another gallon, which soon followed the first lot. The crowd, band and all, was very mellow and happy, and disposed to continue to rally around the flag. The sun was getting low quite as fast as the crowd was getting high. I wanted the celebration to end, which was not so easy to bring about. I did it by getting the band to strike up "Yankee Doodle" and start away. The crowd followed, in great spirits, leaving the old flag still flying.

CHAPTER TEN

With Abraham Lincoln   1861-1862

SOON after this, the People's Court of Denver quit functioning, owing to an act of Congress, February 28, 1861, that established a judicial system for the territory. It provided for a supreme court presided over by three judges and for an attorney general and a marshal. Inferior courts were to be established by territorial statutes. Congress further provided for a government for the territory of Colorado, and [William] Gilpin was selected by President Lincoln as the new governor. On May 20, as acting chairman of the reception committee,[56] I welcomed the governor who, two years later, was to be one of my opponents for delegate to Congress.

In midsummer I was nominated for delegate at Golden City by a union of the loyal elements in the territory, both Republican and Democratic, in the Republican convention. Beverly D. Williams, my opponent, was the nominee of a Democratic convention made up of the opponents of the Lincoln administration.[57] At the following election, I won by a good majority of votes and so became the first delegate from the territory of Colorado. This was to the Thirty-seventh Congress.

My wife started with me from Denver on my way to Washington. We were twenty-six days crossing the plains to Nebraska City. There I left my wife with our relatives and went on by water and rail to Washington. I took my seat in the House on December 31, 1861. That same day my son, Hiram Pitt, Jr., was born at Nebraska City. In the following April I went back there and brought my wife and boy to Washington. We took rooms and boarded with Captain Goddard at 511 I Street until the end of my first term in Congress.

In November 1862 I ran for election to the Thirty-eighth Congress, beating by a good plurality J. M Francisco, the Democratic candidate, and ex-governor Gilpin, who bolted the Republican convention. So it was I who was the Colorado delegate all during President Lincoln's first term until March 4, 1865. Throughout my four years service in Congress, I had the pay and all the privileges of a member except that of voting and of being placed on committees of the House. Thus handicapped, I could do little as regards the enactment of laws for the benefit of Colorado. However, I succeeded in getting a branch mint established at Denver, though it was not fitted up for coining.[58] My principal work was done before the Executive Department by getting established post routes and post offices throughout Colorado; also local land offices, military posts, the removal of the surveyor's office from Salt Lake City to Denver, etc.[59]

All the four terrible years of the war, I did my utmost to uphold and sustain President Lincoln's administration. I had never met him before the inauguration, and though myself a lawyer, I had heard little of him in my western home, which was then more remote from Illinois than San Francisco is now from New York. Nor did I give much heed to what little I heard of Mr. Lincoln, even after his nomination and election. Until I met him personally, I did not regard him as much above the average. By no means did I regard him as equal in ability to Seward, whom he had beaten in the contest for the Republican nomination for president. This, however, was the general feeling at the time, and it was for the most part shared by the convention that nominated him. He was not considered to have much intellect or force or worth of character, though all others than the slaveholders believed him honest. The general estimate of his character is evident from the fact that he was familiarly called "Honest Old Abe."

At the risk of repeating much that has already been said of Mr. Lincoln thousands of times, I cannot refrain from giving my own recollections and impressions of him. During my two terms in Congress, I saw much of him both officially and socially, and I could not but regard him then, as ever since, as the greatest and wisest American of the nineteenth century.

He was a big, rawboned man, a very giant in strength; plain of dress and awkward in manner; of moral and manly courage; always kind and considerate of others. In every true quality of manhood, it was said of him that he "never forgot to be a gentleman." It was his character mainly that won him the nomination and the election. He never had been, and never became, rich or very well to do in the money sense of the term; and few knew that he had brains until after he became president.

No man who has occupied that high office ever had to bear so great and so continuous responsibilities as did Mr. Lincoln throughout his entire term of office. Nor has there ever been another president who has performed the duties of his office with such kindness and ability. His rise to fame was more remarkable than that of George Washington in one respect. Washington had the advantages of aristocratic birth and training; Lincoln was born in poverty and reared among the plain, common people.

As to his sagacity, I can cite no more perfect proof than the manner in which he prepared the ground for the Emancipation Proclamation. In September [1862], he warned the southerners that he would proclaim their slaves free unless they ceased fighting the government by the first of the following January. Had he issued the proclamation at once, without this warning, the act would have created great dissatisfaction within our own lives. It is by no means improbable that some of the border states would have rebelled. But by putting the responsibility of the decision on the slaveholders, he avoided condemnation by a strong party in the North who favored slavery yet were opposed to secession. Indeed, at the time of this forewarning, a clear majority of voters in the North were against emancipation. In this way, Mr. Lincoln held together the "Union" supporters of the government; and when the time he had set came without any offer on the part of the secessionists to cease hostilities, a large majority of the North was willing to accept the freeing of the slaves as a war measure.

From the first, Mr. Lincoln had emphasized as his position that his purpose was to save the union of the states. By being reticent about emancipation, he held the support of many Unionists even in the South. Yet I believe that at the time he issued his warning to the slaveholders in September, he had foreseen the necessity of abolishing slavery and was as strongly set in this purpose as any Abolitionist if only for the reason that he realized that such was the only way to preserve the Union. A house divided against itself cannot stand. As he himself put it, "The nation could not continue half free and half slave."[60]

It was my good fortune to have a friendly acquaintance with Gen. J. B. S. Todd, delegate to the Thirty-seventh Congress from the territory of Dakota. He was a cousin of Mr. Lincoln's and on intimate terms with the family, having the entrée of the White House at all hours. Todd's experience in civil and political life was less than mine. As we had much similar business in common for our respective constituents, we frequently conferred and acted in concert. Whenever we had any business with the president, our habit was to prepare our budget and go together to seek an interview.

Knowing the habits of Mr. Lincoln, the general selected the hour of seven in the evening as the best time for our audiences. We would go together to the White House. There the general would lead the way in past the ushers, all of whom he knew, direct to the audience room. This we usually reached just before the president came in after his dinner so that we would be his first callers for the evening. With mankind in general, just after a satisfactory meal is the best time to find anyone in good humor. Mr. Lincoln was no exception to the rule. Not that I ever knew of his being in a rage or passion during all his administration. Yet he could show and express strong indignation when the occasion justified. Even on such occasions, his feelings were kept well in control, like "an iron hand in a velvet glove."

After presenting and getting through with our several matters of business, Todd and I would remain and converse with Mr. Lincoln until some other caller was announced. At such times the president did most of the talking; one of us, usually Todd, striking in now and then with a suggestion to keep him going. It was on such occasions that I saw most of the man himself behind the office.

One time I remember that Todd remarked, "Mr. President, if it is not a state secret, I wish you would tell us why General Butler was removed from Grant's headquarters before Petersburg." Mr. Lincoln uttered a gentle "humph," and after a moment's thought, answered: "Oh, no; it is no state secret at all. All there was about the matter was that Grant thinks he knows more about military matters than Butler— and I guess he *does*. But Butler knows more about everything else. So I suppose it was annoying to Grant to have Butler around the headquarters. He asked Stanton to get Butler away. Stanton did, and that is all there is to it."

I have given the words. But it is impossible to give the inimitable intonations of Mr. Lincoln's voice, the twinkle in his eyes, and the gesture of head and shoulder, as in his quaint manner he revealed the true inwardness of Grant's reason for desiring Butler's removal. General Grant was called the "silent man," and the name was a true one so far as word of mouth was concerned. He preferred to let his acts speak for him. Butler, on the other hand, was a brilliant talker. At the headquarters mess at which the "silent man" presided, Butler just about monopolized the conversation. This was much to the entertainment of all present save the "silent man," whose thoughts were on the problems of war.

At another time, Mr. Lincoln told Todd and myself all about the conference between Horace Greeley and the Confederate peace commission, which had recently taken place on the Canadian side of Niagara Falls. When the fact of the conference came out, Mr. Greeley had been unmercifully ridiculed by the greater number of the newspapers. This so annoyed him that he published a statement in which he tried to vindicate himself by throwing the entire responsibility on the president.

The facts in the case were, briefly, about as follows: Soon after the beginning of the war, the rebel leaders saw how greatly to their interest it would be to be recognized as belligerents for the purpose of the exchange of prisoners. This would give the Confederate government recognition as a belligerent power. Thereby their cause would be placed on a broader plane and they would be entitled to greater privileges from this and other nations. Such results would have been most perilous to our nation. Mr. Lincoln could not entertain the proposition for a moment. Had he at that time entered into any kind of a treaty or agreement with these ambassadors, other nations would soon have followed his example, and no doubt gone further. It is well known how far England and France went in that direction, even as it was.

So it was mainly for the purpose to gain recognition as an established power that the Confederate peace commission was sent to Niagara Falls to open negotiations with President Lincoln. This he clearly perceived. But Mr. Greeley, being less shrewd and more confiding, thought that the conference would bring about a cessation of hostilities, end of war, and effect a complete reconciliation. With this in mind, he came to the president and asked to be appointed one of a commission to meet and treat with the Confederate commission. This Mr. Lincoln declined to do, giving his reasons. Mr. Greeley admitted they were good and sufficient explanations why the president could not officially send a commission or officially do anything else to recognize the Confederates as a government.

At the same time, Mr. Lincoln said to Greeley that he greatly desired peace, and that personally he would do all in his power to bring it about. He then suggested to Greeley to go and meet the Confederate commission without being officially accredited. As editor of the *Tribune*, then the most influential paper in the United States, this would be very appropriate for him to do, for he was well known all over the country as a peace-loving citizen. For this reason, it might very well happen that he could do something towards bringing about peace. Mr. Greeley proceeded to meet the Confederates on his own responsibility. It is well known, however, that when the commissioners learned that he had no official authority from the president to treat with them, they scorned to have any conference with him. He had to return to New York without having accomplished anything.

During the darkest hours of the war I ever found Mr. Lincoln strong but sad. At such times he was not given to storytelling. But when things were going our way and there was news of victories, the floodgates of his humor would open wide, and there would seem to be no end of his fund of homemade stories, told to illustrate the improved conditions of the war. When he granted a request or petition, he did it promptly and modestly, in a manner to make one think it was but a small thing to do and to be done by him as a matter of course. When, on the other hand, he had to give a denial, it was ever done in the kindest and gentlest manner, very often by means of a humorous anecdote showing the absurdity of the thing asked for in such a manner that it would please and amuse the applicant and leave no grounds for sourness.

His legs and arms were long, and his face and chest somewhat gaunt or emaciated. And yet, with all his homeliness of form and feature, there was nothing whatever repulsive about his looks. On the contrary, there was that in his appearance which invited one's nearer approach and confidence, and the feeling that he would be a "good man to tie to," to use the camp phrase. The more one saw of him, the better he looked. This was so with myself, and many others told me the same. He was so very homely that it made him good-looking.

Of all the eminent men whom I have met during the last half century and more, Mr. Lincoln was the only one who did not grow less the nearer I got to him or the more familiarly I knew him. General Grant is the only other one whom I could name as a good second to Mr. Lincoln in this respect. Years after the war, in 1886 or 1887, I was waiting on business in the lobby of the House of Representatives, just back of the rear seats of the members. Two men nearby, one of whom seemed to be a member, began to talk so distinctly that their conversation was plainly audible above the noise of the House. By their accent, I knew that they were southern men. But I paid no heed to what they said until one of them mentioned the name of Lincoln. Then I heard one of them say: "Fitz Hugh told me the General said that Lincoln was the greatest general of the war."

Just at this point, Judge Symes, then our representative from Colorado, came back to see me. I asked him if he knew the men. He could not give me their names but was certain they were southerners, most likely Virginians. When I told him what I had overheard, he agreed with me it meant that General Robert E. Lee had so expressed himself as to the great military ability of Lincoln, to his nephew, Fitz Hugh Lee. The fact that this happened in the eighties, when there was still a great deal of lingering bitterness in the South, convinces me that the southerner would have been very careful not to misquote what had been told him. If General Robert E. Lee did make the remark, it is worth very serious consideration, for it will be conceded that no American was better qualified to judge of military ability than was General Lee.

CHAPTER ELEVEN

Overland to California   1863

B ACK IN 1845 I had felt a strong desire to go to Oregon in company with some of our Missouri neighbors who were outfitting to go there. Others had gone even before that year. But my ambition to go to school back in Ohio, and then to study law, overcame my urge to see Oregon. Yet I always had a hankering for a trip to the Pacific Coast. At last, in 1863, my opportunity came around through the favor of Mr. Chase, the secretary of the treasury.

Congress had passed an act authorizing the establishment of a mint at Carson City, Nevada Territory. Mr. Chase commissioned me to locate and purchase a site for it.[61] All my traveling expenses were provided for, and I was given my choice of routes going and coming, overland across the plains or around by water and across the Isthmus of Panama. As I wished to pass through Denver, I took the land route, traveling by railroad to its termination at Atchison, Kansas. From that town on west to Sacramento, California, the only public conveyance was the Holliday Overland stage.[62]

This coach route covered six hundred miles to Denver. From there it rolled another six hundred to Salt Lake and a third six hundred to Carson City by way of Camp Floyd, Deep Creek, Reese Run, and Virginia City. That made eighteen hundred miles in all, with the Sierras still to be crossed by travelers who wished to go on to the Pacific Coast. It was the old Cherokee Trail that had been traveled in earlier days by Jim Baker and the Cherokees with their pack train. My company during the long coach ride was the Episcopal bishop [Joseph Cruikshank] Talbot. As at the time many Indians were on the warpath, we were both armed. The bishop had a Navy revolver; I had the same and also a double-barreled shotgun.

Sunday morning, after leaving Denver, I was on the boot with the driver when the bishop called out hurriedly to halt the coach and for me to hand him my gun. This was all said and done in a jiffy, and the bishop fired from inside the coach. His shot killed a mountain grouse. Both the driver and myself were greatly relieved when we learned that the bishop was not shooting Indians or holdups. But the driver did not forget to let the bishop hear from him that it was "wicked to hunt on Sunday." The good bishop asserted that it was done in his diocese, and, anyhow, "it should not count this one."

Our trip to Carson City took seventeen days in all, the coach being on the road night and day. Most of our meals came out of lunch baskets. This was hardly as comfortable or expeditious as traveling nowadays in a Pullman Palace car with a diner on the train, but it beat walking or riding behind an ox team. At old Fort Bridger, Utah, I stopped over a coach to visit Judge Carter, with whom I spent a very agreeable day. His hospitable bed and board were of great relief to me after the fatigue of my long ride and the unpalatableness of dry lunch-basket fare.

The coach by which I was to continue my journey the next day reached Fort Bridger late in the afternoon, and it did not leave until a little before sunset. As all the inside seats were occupied, I had to ride outside with the driver. In good weather and with good roads, this is the best seat on a coach. Under favorable circumstances, it was always much sought after by passengers. The decision lay with the driver, and I am pleased to testify that I never knew a good driver who did not pick out the best looking lady to sit with him on the boot in preference to any man. On this occasion, however, matters were different, the inside seats being, as I have said, all occupied, and there were no ladies among the passengers. For another thing, having before them the cold night's ride across the mountains, the passengers had all concluded that the inside of the coach would be more comfortable than the top. So I was elected to the seat outside with the driver.

As we were about to start, Judge Carter handed me a bottle of whiskey toddy with the remark that I would need it to keep myself warm through the night. The driver was quite interested. In those [days] the average stage driver kept eyes, ears, and mouth open at all times, eager and ready to "take suthin." I stowed the bottle on my side of the seat, and off we started. For the first six miles the road was a heavy upgrade and the four-mule team walked slowly. The driver dozed much of the time. But I was wakeful, being chilled by the cool night air and worried by our tedious progress. The six-mile climb to the top took six hours.

Just before reaching the summit, I felt I must have something to cheer me up. As I never liked to drink alone, I roused the driver by proposing a drink. He awakened on the instant, very willing to join me. While we sampled the judge's toddy, we entered into a "hoss" talk. That is always an interesting subject to a stage driver. But when you talk hoss to a *mule* driver, you had better not know too much yourself, as I soon learned. I expressed a very decided opinion that mules were too "pokey" for a stage team and that the company ought to furnish horses for this mountain division.

The driver said nothing until we had taken another drink. He then replied, with all the gravity due to his position and the subject: "Look here, stranger, you don't know nothing about staging. Mules are a damn sight better nor horses in the mountains, and don't you forget it. When we git to the top of this ridge, you'll see. Watch the ears of the off lead when I yell 'Pete' and stamp on the boot. You'll see. Here, let's have another drink. We're about up."

Just as he finished his drink we reached the summit. Though it was now too dark to see ahead, the driver knew the road, which here stretched out before us smooth and level for half a mile or so along the mountain ridge. He yelled "Pete!" and stamped on the boot. The mules started off like shot off a shovel, whirling us along on a dead run. The driver nudged me with his elbow and shouted: "Didn't I tell you? Look at Pete's ears. They're going like a pair of shears." I took his word for this, as it was too dark for me to see Pete's ears, or much of either of the leaders.

At the end of the level stretch the road turned abruptly to the left, down the steep, rocky side of the ridge into the valley. This was the old road. But recently a new road had been made down the mountainside a few rods short of the old descent, and this cutoff was little less steep and rocky. In the darkness and the excitement of our mad race along the ridge, the driver either forgot or failed to notice the cutoff until we were right upon the turn into it. He tugged hard on the left reins and brought the mules suddenly around. The coach swung around after them, all but toppling over. Before the driver could get his foot on the brake, we were plunging down the mountainside at [an] unabated pace. I was violently jostled and jerked about by the bounding of the coach over the rocks, and cried out to the driver my danger of being thrown off the seat. He bade me, with an oath, to hold on to him, which I did.

On we went, plunging down the hill at breakneck speed. All the time the passengers inside were yelling at the driver. They were being tumbled about together worse than I was outside—to all of which the driver paid not the slightest heed. He kept right on at the same pace for a quarter mile or more before we reached the foot of the steep slope. From there he raced on, up a smooth stretch of gently ascending road to the Quaking Asp station. We arrived in record time with a well-winded team but all passengers still aboard.

Before the driver got down off the boot, he turned to me and said: "Well now, stranger, can a mule team travel fast enough over a mountain road to suit you?" I replied with emphasis that they could and was relieved when he forgot to propose another drink. I felt sure he had had quite enough. At this station Pete and his mates were exchanged for another mule team. The driver told me that these fresh animals were a damned poor, bunged-up lot and that downhill was the place to make time with a mule. When we started on, he ran them all the way down the canyon to the Bear Creek station. This was the end of his division. I very gladly took a parting drink with him and said good-bye.

Here the mules were exchanged for a team of California horses, and our new driver, Pete McManus, took us on down Echo Canyon, over a smooth road at a rattling pace. The last ten miles were covered in fifty-five minutes. This was the most delightful part of the coach ride on the entire trip.

At Salt Lake City I overtook Bishop Talbot, my fellow traveler from Denver, with whom I had parted company and laid over a day at Fort Bridger. We put up at the Salt Lake House. The short stopover confirmed my unfavorable opinion of Mormonism as then practiced, for polygamy was general throughout Utah. When in riding around the city I spoke out my feelings about this and about Brigham Young, the driver of the carriage looked no little alarmed and sought to hush me.

After bathing in Great Salt Lake at Black Rock and looking about the city another day, the good bishop and I resumed our journey. We had restocked our lunch baskets with boiled beef and sheep tongues, diverse bottles of claret wine, and two bottles of cognac. On this trip I learned to appreciate claret. The bitter, brackish water most of the way—and the alkali dust all the way—made the acid of the wine almost a necessity for the five hundred miles between Salt Lake City, Utah, and Virginia City, Nevada.

The trip across the desert was monotonous and dreary all the way. It was without any incident worthy to note, though we had grave reason to apprehend trouble from the Indians. The Gosiutes,[63] very recently on the warpath, had just been pacified by a treaty made with them by Governor Doty.[64] We met the governor and his party returning from the conference. He told us that peace had been concluded but that we had better be on the alert. We were all armed. I had, as I have told, a Colt's Navy revolver and a double-barreled shotgun; the bishop had his revolver and a prayer book; the driver a gun and two revolvers.

The so-called Gosiute war, just concluded by this treaty, had lasted only a month or two. Yet during that brief time the Indians, to cite one instance, had taken a stagecoach, killing the driver and three passengers. And all along, for two hundred miles of the route, they had waylaid other stages, shooting from ambush and killing most of their victims at the first fire. All told, several drivers and passengers and stage horses had been killed or wounded. In another instance, the Indians laid [sic] in a small gully near a station. Early in the morning, when the two stock tenders brought the horses out of the stable to groom them, the Gosiutes shot both men, killing one and wounding the other. The latter was able to escape by springing on the horse he was leading out by the halter.

He fled down the road as fast as the animal could run. The Indians fired a shower of bullets after him, but none hit either him or the horse. About four miles along the road, the poor fellow met a party of immigrants. He started to tell what had happened. In the midst he fell from his horse and died. He had ridden all that distance with a mortal wound. The immigrants placed his body in their wagon and advanced cautiously to the station. They found the buildings a heap of burning ruins, the horses run off by the Indians, and the corpse of the other stock tender scalped and mutilated. At the time I passed this place, the ashes and charred logs of the burned stable were still lying about the new building.

Some forty or fifty miles beyond this station, as I rode beside the driver down a narrow canyon three or four miles long, I noticed a half-healed wound on the rump of the team's off leader, a spirited mare. I asked the driver about it. He answered: "Indians—about four weeks ago. Just you keep your eye on the mare. She'll tell you when we reach the spot where she got that shot." About a mile farther on, we were swinging along at the ordinary stage gait of six miles an hour. Suddenly the mare sprang forward in fright, turning her head to look up the side of the mountain.

"Here," said the driver, pointing with his whip-stock. "Here's the place. The Injins fired on the stage from behind that dike of black rock you see up thar. They killed Eagan, a passenger who was beside me on the boot right where you sit, and wounded the mare, all at the first fire. We got away, though, before they got in another shot, for I tell you, stranger, the team needed no whip to do their best down this smooth road. They was as badly skeered as I was, you bet.

"Eagan died down thar in the boot before we reached the next station. The shot that killed him must have passed just back of my left shoulder, for it hit him in the right side, pretty high up, and come from my side of the road at a point forty or fifty feet above us. Before he died, he said the shot must have been aimed at me.

"If they'd got me, or disabled the mare, the team would've stopped, or else run off and wrecked things generally. Either way, the Injins would've captured the whole outfit, which, as Eagan said, they no doubt thought to do. As it was, they only killed him. They didn't get his scalp, nor even know they's killed him and wounded the mare. After firing at us, and we got off, the cowardly assassins fled up the mountain."

At Deep Creek was what was called a home station, where several employees were always to be found. Eight miles west of there was a small, lone station on a smooth ridge in sight from Deep Creek station, to which the road ran from it on a smooth downgrade. It was as nice a natural road as one could wish to see. The next station was thirty-five miles distant, the longest route for one team on the entire line but made necessary by the lack of water between. As a matter of course, the company had their best teams on this long route. Only the very best of horses could travel at the rate of six miles an hour for that distance without water and haul a heavy load of passengers, as was frequently required.

One afternoon, during the same Gosiute war, the coach from the west came dragging up to the lone station eight miles west of Deep Creek. The horses were sweating and tired by their long thirty-five-mile pull. The stable at this place was so situated that the stage had to pass between it and the cabin of the stock tenders and there stop for the change of teams. It was the custom, whenever a stage came in sight of a station, for the stock tenders to throw the harness on the fresh team and stand ready to put them to the coach as soon as the incoming team could be released. But on this afternoon the driver saw no signs of life about the place. Being on the outlook for Indians, he suspected that something might be wrong. So he drove up very slowly, keeping his eyes open.

On the boot beside the driver sat one of the passengers, a man from Iowa. Inside were the man's son, a boy of sixteen, and Judge Mott,[65] then delegate to Congress from Nevada Territory. Just as the coach reached the usual stopping place, the doors of the stable were thrown open. A number of Indians who had been waiting in ambush mounted on the relay stage horses, fired a volley at the coach, and charged out yelling.

At the sound of the guns, the tired coach team dashed off at a dead run down the smooth grade towards the Deep Creek station. The first shots had wounded both the driver and the Iowa man but had failed to hit the two inside passengers or any of the horses. The Indians, mounted on the fresh horses, soon came up behind and on each side of the coach, yelling and firing at both men and animals. Fortunately none of the latter were disabled, and the noise frightened them into still greater speed.

Shortly after the first volley, the Iowa man fell forward, apparently dead. He would have fallen off the coach had not the driver thrown out his left foot and slid the body down into the front boot of the coach. At the same time he urged the team to their utmost speed to keep ahead of the Indians. Thus they went racing for life down the long grade to the Deep Creek station—which all the time was in plain view.

When about half the distance had been covered, the driver called out to Judge Mott, who was shooting at the Indians from inside the coach, to come up quick. The judge climbed out on the side of the swaying coach, where he was exposed to the fire of the savages. But he safely reached the vacant seat beside the driver. The latter very deliberately handed him the reins and whip. Telling him to lay it on the wheelers, he slowly slid himself down into the boot, beside the body of the Iowa man.

On they whirled in their terrible race, the pursued wild with fear, the Indians wild with the bloodthirsty joy of the chase and eager to take the scalps of their victims. They kept coming at full gallop until within gunshot distance of the Deep Creek station. Then, seeing the whites at the station running out with their guns, the cowardly savages wheeled about and rode away without trying to destroy the station.

Very soon afterwards, coach and all reached the station. The Iowa man, though still unconscious, was found to have been only slightly wounded. But the brave driver was dead. He no doubt knew that he was dying when he called up Judge Mott and so deliberately gave him the lines and slid down into the boot. By his coolness and fortitude, he saved the lives of his companions and cheated the Indians of his scalp, which last was considered quite a point, even among the whites, in the grim game of Indian warfare.

I was told this story by the driver who had been put on the Deep Creek route in place of the slain man and drove the same coach over the long desert haul. He concluded the account a short time before we reached the station eight miles west of Deep Creek. It was late on [a] September night, and the air in the valleys was chilly. As I sat beside him on the boot, I was shaking with cold and fear—perhaps both.

Well, when we reached this station where the Indians had made their attack, all was dark and cold. I could not help thinking of the driver's account of what had happened here only four weeks before. The stock tenders, lanterns in hand, at once came out of the stable to change teams. I asked one of them if I could get to a fire to warm myself for the brief stop. He told me yes, to go into the cabin but to be quick about it.

There was no light in the cabin, he said. But if I went in and straight across from the door, I'd find the fireplace and some dry willow brush on the left side of it. By raking open the coals and ashes, I could start a blaze in a minute with the dry brush leaves. This I proceeded to do in a hurry, for I had no time to spare. Very shortly I had a handful of brush on the hearth blazing up and lighting the whole room. I crouched before it, watching the flames and holding out my benumbed hands to them.

Suddenly on my right, an Indian, wakened by the bright light, raised himself up from the corner near the fireplace. With the full light on his hideous face, he stared at me with, as I thought, a ferocious look. My hair stood up so stiffly that it nearly pushed off my hat. I sprang about and rushed back to my seat on the coach without stopping to talk to anybody. I had no need of the fire, for I was hot with fright. After the stage driver's story, the sight of that Gosiute was quite enough Indian experience for one night.

These accounts of recent murders by the Indians by no means lessened the hardships of the trip. But I managed to get across the desert in fairly good shape, thanks to the company of the good bishop. He was a most patient, cheerful, and courageous traveler. While stopping over in Virginia City for a day's rest, we went together through the

Sutro Tunnel into the Comstock Mine. This we found almost hot enough to bake bread as we stood for a few moments before the breast of bright ore seven feet thick.

At Carson City, after locating the site for the branch mint, and while waiting to get the title deeds to the ground from the absent lot owners, I took the opportunity to run over the mountains to California. I went by coach over what was called the Kingsbury grade. It was a roadbed cut zigzag for three miles or more out of the side of a mountain that stood at an angle of about forty degrees. The road was wide enough for two teams to pass, though in many places with no more than a few feet to spare. This grade extended from the town of Austin up to the summit near Lake Bigler on the Sierra Range.

The outfit with which I traveled consisted of three large Troy coaches, each carrying twenty passengers and much silver bullion, and drawn by six fine, large American horses. The driver of the leading coach was Hank Monk, who was celebrated for his drive with Horace Greeley over this road three years before. The account of it from Monk reminded me of my experience with the mule team. Mr. Greeley was the only passenger in the coach, and he was due to arrive in San Francisco on a certain near date. Starting up the heavy grade from Austin, the team had to proceed at a walk, with frequent stops to blow. This made Mr. Greeley very restless and impatient lest he should not reach San Francisco in time. Every now and then he called out to the driver to whip up and get along faster. Though greatly annoyed, Monk kept his temper. He patiently replied that he could get his passenger through on time.

At last they reached the summit. Then Monk turned loose. Down the other side was a long, rocky descent, and the horses took it at an unusually fast gait. As they thundered down the rough grade, the coach swayed and jarred over the stones while inside Mr. Greeley was tumbled about from side to side and from end to end, his head now and then whacking up against the top. He called out to the driver to go slower over such a bad road. But Monk pretended to think he was being urged to hurry on. At each call from Greeley, Monk cracked his whip and shouted back for him not to worry, that he would get him through on time. He kept this up for several miles until they were down the mountain and in the valley. Mr. Greeley was all but bruised to a jelly—but he reached San Francisco on time.

Our first meal out from Austin was noon dinner at Lake Tahoe. The like of that dinner I never saw before or since. There was a long table set with places for all our crowd, and we numbered more than sixty. The table was laden with a great abundance of meats, vegetables, breads, pies, sauces, and fruits. All the courses and the dessert—in addition, several vases of flowers—had been crowded upon the table together. About every five feet, down the entire length of the great board, was a large platter stacked high with fried speckled trout that had been freshly caught from Lake Tahoe, nearby the hotel. When we reboarded our coaches after this spread, it was found that the seats were more crowded than before. At least, this was so in my case.

That night we took supper at Strawberry station. The hotel was so called because the proprietor's name was Berry and because he gave the freighters, as forage for their teams, straw instead of hay. An all-night ride brought us to Lincoln. We barely had time there for breakfast before taking the cars down to Sacramento, twenty miles farther. From Sacramento the last part of the trip to San Francisco was made by steamboat down the Sacramento River and the Bay. This was a delightful trip and a great relief from the fatigue of the day and night riding in the stage.

It was the driest part of the year in California.[66] As we passed down the river, I could look for miles out from the hurricane deck of the boat. But in no direction could I see aught of green grass or foliage other than a few scattered clumps of cottonwood trees and willow brush along the bank. Otherwise the entire landscape was bare of vegetation, and brown and bare as a fallow field. This first view of coastal California greatly disappointed me. From early boyhood I had in my imagination pictured the Golden State as being verdant and flowery, basking in golden sunshine and balmy breezes. But these scenes from the deck of the steamboat dispelled once and forever my boyhood visions of the green and golden shores of the Pacific and quite disgusted me with the country.

For four days I stopped in San Francisco, except for a visit to Oakland and its suburbs. The roads were everywhere ankle-deep in dust. There was dust everywhere in and around Oakland, settling on and covering everything—buildings, fences, foliage, fruit, and flowers. In my sightseeing I visited the old Spanish mission of San Dolores. It was then a suburb of San Francisco about three miles from the Russ House, where I put up. Another place that I went to see was a resort called the Willows. It was a tract of low ground, several acres in extent, and covered with a growth of willows twelve or fifteen feet in height. Among this growth were pathways and seats. The breeze, circulating beneath the foliage, made it a cool, shady and delightful place in which to pass the heat of the day. In the midst was a large frame building where theatricals were given. In another part of the grounds was a zoological garden. The Willows was near the San Dolores Mission.

A trip out to the Cliff House gave me my first view of the open ocean. It was a grand sight and lost nothing by reason of the seal rock, lying within gunshot, with the thousands of sea lions swimming about them or basking on their ledges. To me it was a wonderful sight. For company I had Mr. Denio of the San Francisco mint. After taking in the view from the Cliff House, we drove along the beach some three or four miles to the Ocean House. As we wheeled along over the hard sand, great waves twenty feet high would come rolling menacingly inshore and break within a few feet of us, the water from the surf spreading up under and beyond our carriage. The water would then recede, only to come up again the next half minute as another roller broke. It gave me the impression that we were traveling lengthwise in a trough of the sea. This was not far from being true—only a matter of a few yards.

On the whole, despite the dryness of the season, I had a most enjoyable time. Though I met few old acquaintances, they were all most cordial. No less so were the new acquaintances I had the pleasure of meeting. There was no need to look for their hearts in their jackets; they carried them "on their sleeves." Among my old friends was Mr. Sargent,[67] one of the California representatives to Congress whom I had known in Washington. He pressed me to stay over until November and then return to Washington with him by way of Panama. I declined for two very good reasons. The first was that I had business to attend to in Denver on my return trip; the second, that the ocean looked so wet that I was most afraid to trust myself to it.

From San Francisco I crossed back over the Sierras by the Truckee stage route to Carson City. There I closed the deal for the block of ground which I had selected for the site of the mint. With the title papers in my carpetbag I continued east on my way overland by coach, as I had come, through all the dust and dangers, the fatigue and deprivations—yet which counted as nothing against the perils of an ocean voyage.

The day before reaching Salt Lake City, on this return trip, we came to a point in sight of and about eight miles northwest of Provo City. At this place, a few weeks before, the Gosiutes had captured a coach. They had killed the driver and four passengers and scattered the contents of the mailbags all over the ground. Many scraps of paper, letters, etc., were still to be seen when we passed.

The Indians had come up through Provo and told the Mormons that they were going to take the "paper wagon" that afternoon. With the stage horses and their harness, all the baggage, and the five scalps, they returned through Provo the same evening. They exhibited their plunder to the Mormons and told what they had done. The latter had seen a part of the massacre through field glasses. Yet they had neither sought to prevent nor to punish the Indians for the bloody work. Though this virtually made them accessories to the murders, I never heard that many of them were called to account for their failure to intervene.

Much to my relief, the Gosiutes were no longer on the warpath, and the Utes in Colorado were peaceful. This meant safety from Salt Lake City to Denver. But while I had been away, the Plains Indians between Denver and the Missouri River had become very hostile. The red warriors had become very active in attacking coaches and emigrant trains. Coming west I had taken coach at Atchison, as I have told. But the Indians had made this route south of the Platte so hot that part of the way the coaches had been shifted to the north of that river, with the eastern terminus at Omaha. From Denver the route still ran down the south side of the Platte, but it crossed over at Julesburg. From there the travel proceeded cautiously down the north side.

Going over even this new and safer route was little better than "running the gauntlet." Between some of the stations the danger was so great that passengers had to give tips to drivers to induce them to proceed even in daytime. Even the boldest could not be induced to travel at night. For more than half the distance from Denver to the Missouri the odds were about even that at almost any difficult part of the road Indians would swoop down on the coach and wipe out the party. With the drivers it was not a question of screwing up courage to make a single trip through this dangerous country. They had to stay for weeks in the midst of the danger, driving back and forth on their exposed routes.

As a class, those stage drivers from 1860 to 1869 showed a courage and daring not surpassed by soldiers who charge a redoubt. I should say that they showed even greater courage in sticking to their posts. For it is the long, continued strain of daily and hourly peril that is most likely to break a man's nerve. I am thankful to be able to say that we rode through to Omaha without sighting, much less being attacked, by the roving bands of Plains Indians.

CHAPTER TWELVE

Washington Farewell 1864-1865

EARLY in 1865, near the end of my second term in Congress, George K. Otis brought me a message which was a joint resolution of the legislature of Colorado Territory. By it I was instructed to apply to the president to place General [Patrick Edward] Connor in command of the military district of Colorado. This was less than two months after the so-called battle of Sand Creek, where a force under command of Col. [John] Chivington had slaughtered Black Kettle's band of Cheyennes, including the women and children. That massacre had greatly enraged the Plains Indians and had set them to raiding all the roads to Colorado and about the border settlements. They killed and scalped travelers and settlers whenever they could, burned the homes of outlying settlers, and drove off their cattle and horses. The white men had resorted to Indian methods of warfare, and the Indians retorted with interest, sparing neither sex nor age.

Upon receiving the resolution of the Colorado legislature, I at once went to the Executive Mansion and stated the matter to Mr. Lincoln. He gave me a note to Mr. Stanton, the secretary of war. The latter, in turn, ever ready and prompt on matters of importance, told me that the business must first go before the general of the army. With that, he handed me an order for passage on a government transport to the headquarters of General Grant, then at Crown Point on the Mames River. This was also Grant's base of supplies. From it a railroad ran out to the front, eight miles distant, to where Grant's army had invested Petersburg and where it menaced Lee's army, both sides being strongly entrenched.

The transport was booked to leave the evening of the day on which I saw the secretary. So with Otis, whom I had had included in the order, I hurried down to the Potomac and aboard the vessel, just in time. The next morning, about nine, we made the landing at City Point. The quarters of the officers were a cluster of rude log houses built of small pine trunks and without porches, paint, or ornament of any kind. They were, however, all new and neat in appearance, standing here and there among the scattered trees.

Upon my inquiry, the guard pointed out to me Colonel Brown, Grant's adjutant, standing nearby with a group of other officers. I made known to him my desire to see the general on important business. I stated who I was and explained that I had been directed by the secretary of war to see the general. He told me to wait a minute and walked on ahead to one of the cabins that stood apart from the others. This he entered. After a few moments he came out and back to us with the information that the general would see us at once. He added that we could walk over and knock, and then walk right in without need of any introduction.

So Otis and I went over and knocked as directed. A voice said, "Come in." I pushed open the door and stepped inside, Otis following. As I entered, the general was writing at a plain pine table to my right and did not see me until he had turned partly around. He then immediately arose, and I, after introducing myself officially as a member of Congress, introduced Mr. Otis. The general shook hands with us and slowly turned back to his seat. As he sat down again, he extended his hand and caught up a number of dark Havana cigars lying loose upon the rough little table. These he offered to us with an invitation to smoke. We accepted the cigars without need of urging.

To meet officially the general of the army of the United States at the time when he was winning his way against his great opponent was a real honor to anyone, and we were still further favored by the pleasure of a social smoke with him. After a few moments, the general, in his quiet manner, showed by his look that he was ready to hear our business. He listened very carefully while I, as briefly as I could, explained the purpose of my visit. When I had ended, he said, in his quiet, careful way: "I have heard of Sand Creek, and I can but regard that as a massacre."

I replied that we probably would not disagree as to that. Whether Sand Creek was a glorious victory over hostile Indians or a massacre of a friendly band, to our great discredit, the more important and pressing aspect of the affair was its effect on the other Indians. As a result of the fight, hundreds of Sioux, Cheyennes, and Arapahos had gone on the warpath and were committing depredations on the plains east of the mountains. I then explained to him that the Colorado legislature had recommended that Colonel Connor of the California

Volunteers, who was then in Utah, should be put in command of the District of Colorado to succeed Colonel Chivington.

To this the general answered: "I don't know Colonel Connor. The man I would send is General Crook. But I can't spare him." He hesitated a moment, then added, "I will take the matter up, and you will hear of the result through the secretary of war."[68] Though not quite satisfied with this, as I thought he should have said what he would do, I did not consider it courteous to press him further. As we rose to leave, Otis struck in and asked the general for a pass to the front at Petersburg. Without speaking, the general turned to his pen. After spoiling a half sheet of note paper, he wrote out a pass for us on another half sheet. We thanked him, shook hands, and left.

Less than a half hour later, we were with a friend of Otis, a quarter-master, out on the front before Petersburg. We spent a most interesting day along the lines. Among other incidents, we viewed an extensive part of the Confederate lines from a deserted mansion on our picket line. In the afternoon we returned to the river in time to catch our boat for the trip back to Washington. We reached there early the next morning. As we boarded a streetcar after landing, I bought a newspaper. One of the first items that caught my eye was the announcement of the appointment by General Curtis, then in command of the Department of the Missouri, of Colonel Connor to the command of the District of Colorado. In his military life General Grant was a man of few promises but of prompt action—of few words but many deeds.

On the fourth of March 1865, when my second term as delegate to Congress terminated, Mr. Lincoln was inaugurated for his second term as president. Arrangements had been made for the ceremony to be performed at noon on a temporary platform built out from the porch on the east side of the Senate wing of the Capitol. A few minutes before noon, the members of both houses of Congress assembled in the Senate Chamber to witness the inauguration of Andrew Johnson to the office of vice president. When the presiding officer of the Senate rose to administer the oath of office, Mr. Johnson also rose, and standing at the secretary's desk before the chair of the presiding officer, he immediately and unexpectedly began to speak.

No speeches were called for from Mr. Johnson or anyone else. When, without waiting for the administration of the oath, he began to speak, the interruption in the proceedings put all present into a trepidation lest the inauguration of Mr. Lincoln be delayed. Mr. Johnson's face was flushed and his voice not very clear. His speech lasted, I should say, about two minutes. It was cut short by the manner of, and perhaps a whisper from, the over-leaning presiding officer.

The oath was at once administered to Mr. Johnson. All present then hastily went out upon the platform. Mr. Lincoln sat there surrounded by his cabinet officers, the judges of the Supreme Court and other high officers, and by many foreign ministers. It was now twelve o'clock noon. Salmon P. Chase, chief justice of the Supreme Court, immediately administered to Mr. Lincoln the oath of office for his second term—a term which, in less than forty days, was to be cut short by his assassination.

As soon as he had taken the oath, Mr. Lincoln stepped forward to the front of the platform. He there delivered from manuscript his great inaugural address to the immense audience that covered several acres of the street and open ground on the east side of the Capitol. His manner was easy and natural; not aggressive, nor imposing, nor graceful. Yet as he stood there before us, there was that about him both grand and majestic. His address was not lengthy, and there was nothing oratorical in the tone or manner of its delivery. He spoke in a strong voice, not sonorous or musical, but plain and clear. Mr. Lincoln was far less eloquent in public address than when telling his inimitable stories and anecdotes. His great speeches, like those of Edmund Burke, give far more satisfaction when read than when orated. His Gettysburg speech elicitated [sic] no applause when delivered. Yet it gave him worldwide reputation when published and read.

This second inaugural speech called forth little applause at the time, though I believe that it is an even greater one than the Gettysburg speech. It affected me very deeply as I stood listening to Mr. Lincoln deliver it. Nothing loftier has been written than its divine phrase that so aptly sums up the sublime character of the man who wrote it—"With malice against none, and with charity for all."[69]

After the expiration of my second term in Congress, I moved with my family to New Brunswick, New Jersey. There in company with S. F. Knuckolls, a Nebraska friend, I opened an office at 100 Broadway, New York. For a twelvemonth we dealt in Colorado mines and West Virginia oil lands, though with little success. In July of that year, 1865, we bid off a hundred head of mules at the government sale in Washington City. Mr. Knuckolls shipped the animals to Nebraska, and we made a handsome profit on the deal.

While still living at New Brunswick, I took my mother on a visit to Chesterville, Maine, where she was born. This was thirty-four years after our family had left there by wagon to emigrate to Ohio in 1831. On this return, we traveled by railroad, passing through New York City, Boston, and Portland, Maine. At the latter place we changed cars to a line running to Farmington and left the train at Livermore Falls, about 4:00 P.M. After supper there, we started in a two-seated spring wagon for Chesterville. Mother and I were on the back seat, and the driver on the front. He drove at a brisk trot.

After about half a mile, he turned square off to the left, near the bank of a river that we had come in sight of a few minutes before. Up to this time I had seen nothing that I recognized. But just as our wagon turned, I twisted half about to take a last look at the beautiful river. That glance brought to memory the ferry on the Androscoggin River, where we had crossed it thirty-four years before. Sure enough, it was the same place and river and ferry. All looked just as it was pictured in my memory so long past, when I was only five years old.

We were now on the old ridge road to Chesterville. I recalled every turn of it and the hill, and so did Mother. We recognized also the old post-and-rail fence along the road on Grandfather Bradbury's farm. It was still standing in nearly as good condition as it was when we left in 1831. It was built of cedar posts and chestnut rails, which, you must know, make a fence that lasts forever. As the Yankee youth told the stranger, "This is a fact, for Daddy has tried it three times." Riding along the fence, Mother was greatly interested, recognizing everything she saw. Suddenly she nudged me and pointed across a little creek towards a side hill, green-grassed and speckled with dandelions. "See there," she said, "they have gone and spilled over that great stone I used to play on with the schoolchildren when I was a little girl."

Grandfather and Grandmother Bradbury had long since died, and the place had passed into another's ownership. But the old house was there, to all appearances the same as when we had left it so many years before. So also was Grandfather Elisha Bennet's house. It was more than seventy-five years old. Yet it looked brighter and newer in every way than a frame house like it in the Far West after standing five years. Grandfather and Grandmother Bennet both died before we left Maine. I don't remember ever having seen either of them.

We reached my Uncle Rubin Lowell's place before sundown. His wife Lois was my mother's sister. The next day I visited Farmington, where we lived from shortly after I was born until we emigrated to Ohio. Our old red house there was still standing and occupied. Fairbanks Hill, the Pond, and Townsends Tanyard, across, were also still there. But the entire place—houses, mill pond and every other bit of scenery—looked to me small and crowded closely together. On the next Sunday, Uncle Rubin and I drove up to Carthage through a drizzling rain. There we visited my cousin Harrison Storer and his mother, my mother's oldest sister. She was then quite old but strong and active, attending to household duties for four generations of her family, including herself, then living with her or visiting.

Shortly after my visit to Carthage I returned to New Brunswick. But Mother remained in Maine some months visiting with her two sisters. While returning, she visited my cousin Hannah Bradbury Goodman at Charlestown, near Boston, for several days.

CHAPTER THIRTEEN

Utes and Vigilantes 1866-1873

IN 1866 I returned with my family to Denver and resumed the practice of law. The same year the federal authorities instructed Governor Cummings of Colorado Territory and Superintendent of Indian Affairs to effect a treaty with the Uintah band of the Ute Indians. This band claimed all the mountains and country between Green River on the west and the foothills on the east side of the Rockies. Major D. C. Oakes was government agent of these Indians, and old Jim Baker served as interpreter. They were ordered to go over to Middle Park and call the Indians to meet the governor in big council at some point near the Hot Sulphur Springs for the purpose of making a treaty. The governor and party were to follow later with presents.

As secretary of the commission, I accompanied Oakes and Jim. We traveled and camped together for three weeks while notifying the Indians. When the Utes gathered to take part in the proposed treaty council, we were joined by Governor Cummings and his party of about twenty-five men, including A. C. Hunt, afterwards governor.

Among the Indians were many renegade Utes from Utah who came accompanied by Satan—in spirit, if not in the flesh. These at once proceeded to stir up bad blood against our party among the other bands present. There were between three and four hundred Indians at the council, all fully armed. Our party numbered only about twenty-five, and few of us had guns. Old Colorow and his band stood in with the renegades from Utah and was no less ugly and lawless. But the old fraud was not popular with the other prominent Utes, who were better and more peacefully disposed than was he. He was very much put out because they would not take him into caucus with them at the council.

On the second day of the conference, Colorow got together his friends and followers and took up a position a little apart from the main body in clear view of our party. In the midst of the talk, which was being held between Governor Cummings and the group of chiefs, Colorow yelled from the rear of the crowd with menacing gestures towards where Jim Baker and the governor stood. Old Jim seized his rifle from the foot of a tree nearby and made ready for action. He was the only one of our party that had a weapon at hand. The clear intent of Colorow was to incite a massacre. Even had all of us been armed, we could not have hoped to withstand such overpowering numbers of Indians. It was an extremely critical moment. Had a single shot been fired, we would all have been killed and scalped in short order.

But the old scoundrel had been yelling for only a few seconds when Ankatosh, the head chief of all bands present, called out in a still louder voice. Colorow immediately fell silent and slunk back into the midst of his followers. The danger was over almost before we could realize what was happening. But had it not been for the quick, stern interruption of the head chief, Colorow would have had a massacre under way in short order. In all likelihood, he and his crowd had planned the affair all out beforehand.

During the negotiations we had distributed fifty beeves and a large quantity of sugar, coffee, and flour among the Utes present to put them in good humor. But the council broke up with them still refusing to dispose of their lands. Nevertheless, we wound up the affair by giving them a big feast of corn meal mush and molasses. That seemed to put even the renegades in a fairly good frame of mind—if one can ever guess what is in the heart of a savage. After the feast was over and the Indians had left, Baker told us what Colorow had yelled. The words were: "Take the scalp of old Jim and of every white face here!" To this the powerful chief Ankatosh had rejoined, "You get away quick, or I take *your* scalp!"

Later on the Indians again went into conference with the governor. They were, however, slow to talk treaty. They grew more and more sullen and adverse to making any agreements. When at last all the presents had been distributed and the beef herd of fifty fat beeves nearly consumed, they said they would make no treaty at all. Some of the chiefs showed signs of hostility by ordering off the camp followers of our party from fishing in the creek hard by the camp and from taking any photographs of the trees, the creeks, the country, or the Indians. At last Governor Cummings decided it was no use to try further treating with them. He ordered his help to break camp for the return to Denver. While this was being done, the Indians assembled in a close group nearby. The governor gave them a final talk, but it was without any effect. After that there was nothing for us to do but go back home without any treaty.

After Governor Cummings's failure in 1866 to get a treaty with the Colorado Utes, another attempt was made in the winter of 1867–68. This took place at Washington. I went on as a member of the commission headed by Governor A. C. Hunt. Other members were my friends Kit Carson, Major D. C. Oakes, and Lafayette Head.[70] Our mutual friend Ouray, that noble head chief of all the Utes, led a large delegation of other chiefs and headmen. Colonel A. G. Boone, a grandson of Daniel Boone, was with us, but U. M. Curtis had succeeded Jim Baker as interpreter. Other chiefs than Ouray were Ankatosh, Piah, Suruipe and Captain Jack. In later years, Jack was the leader in the defeat of Major Thornburgh's command at the time of the Meeker Massacre.

At Washington, the result of our united efforts was a treaty fair alike to the tribe and to the white settlers of Colorado. It established a Ute Indian reservation that covered nearly a fourth of Colorado Territory, along the west side. During this treaty making, Kit Carson was taken sick, owing, I believe, to the damp cold of the eastern climate. Upon our return to Denver, he started south with Major Oakes for his home at Taos, New Mexico. But he became worse and died at Fort Lyon. On the way his trail passed over what is now Daniels Park. Oakes told me it was there that Kit built his last campfire. I went out and found the ashes and bits of burnt wood of the fire and placed on them a small cairn of stones. Later on the site was permanently marked with a bronze tablet.

After General Grant was nominated for the presidency he came out to Denver by way of the Smoky Hill route with Sherman, Sheridan, and Frederick T. Dent. The next day, July 22, they took coach to Central City, then to Georgetown. I rode with them and others on the way to the ascent of Grays Peak, elevation 14,274. At the head of the high gulch where the trail started to zigzag up the steep final ascent, the rest of the party remained in their saddles. I climbed afoot and beat the horses to the top.

In 1867 I suffered the loss of my wife, Sarah McCabe Bennet. She had borne to me six children, the first two of whom died in infancy, and the third, Caroline, at the age of three. But two sons, Hiram Pitt, Jr., and John Bradbury, and a daughter, Sara, survived.[71]

Early in 1869 Clara Ames, granddaughter of Nathaniel Ames, a veteran of the War of the Revolution, was teaching school at the Dry Creek Bridge just north of Petersburg. With another teacher she came to call upon the family of my brother Joseph on a nearby farm. My three children were playing outside the house. While I was talking with the young ladies, four-year-old Johnny began to howl as if hurt. The other teacher sat unmoved. But Miss Ames sprang up and hastened outside to care for and soothe the little boy. That act of kindness and sympathy for a child would, even alone, have been enough to win my regard. I courted and won Clara Ames, and we were married April 16, 1869. She reared the young children of my first wife as her own and bore me a son and daughter, Robert and Blanche.

In March of that year, President Grant had appointed me postmaster of Denver to succeed my friend Andrew Sagendorf. The salary was $4,000 a year. Ed Summer remained as assistant postmaster and Charles R. McCord as clerk. Mails from the south were carried by stage; eastern mails came over the Denver Pacific Railroad, which had just been completed. The post office was located in a room, part of which was used as a book and periodical store. In the summer of 1870 Postmaster Creswell came to Denver, and seeing the cramped quarters of my office, authorized me to secure a better place. I moved the office to the new Hughes Block on the corner of Lawrence and Fifteenth streets. Though I fitted it up with lock and delivery boxes and was allowed additional clerks, it still was not able to handle all the mail properly. Nearly every transient to Colorado had his mail addressed to Denver, thence to be forwarded. As a result, the office was nearly swamped, especially with second-, third-, and fourth-class matter, much of which could not be delivered.

My last experience in helping to avert mob violence was in 1869 or 1870. Dave Cook, then sheriff, had in his custody a prisoner named Griswold, who was charged with murder. One day Griswold, who was lodged in the first county jail on Larimer Street, wantonly killed a fellow prisoner who had been arrested on some trivial charge. The bitter feeling against Griswold created by this second murder was quickly intensified and inflamed to the danger point by the violent comments of the newspapers. Before noon on the day after the murder, a handbill signed by one of the editors was posted around town. It called for a public meeting at two that afternoon at a large store on Market Street to consider the proper course to pursue with Griswold.

It did not take me long to realize this meant the organization of a mob to hang the prisoner. Brutal as was the crime, there was nothing to justify a lynching. By no chance could the prisoner escape from such a man as Sheriff Cook, and there was every reason to believe that he would be duly tried and hanged. I felt it my duty to prevent, if possible, the threatened lynching. Going to our mayor, John Harper, I told him what was in the wind and asked him, as mayor of the city, to take steps to stop the contemplated violence. He thought I must be mistaken in my suspicions and said he thought it hardly worth while to pay any attention to the meeting or give it any official notice. Yet he agreed with me that if a mob was formed and a lynching did take place, it would be a disgrace and an injury to the city in the minds of eastern people.

With this I left him and returned to the post office. A little before two o'clock I saw a lot of men standing together near the jail, down towards Fourteenth Street. Among them was the man who had signed the call for the meeting. Perceiving that they meant business in short order, I hastened down to fetch the mayor. We managed to reach the place of meeting a few steps in advance of the crowd. We went into the hall with the crowd just behind us. I have no doubt they thought we were in sympathy with their intended action.

There was no one before us in the hall. It was quite bare other than for a pile of short boards and shavings at the upper end and a long workbench standing against the side wall a short distance from the front entrance. Upon this bench I climbed at once, while the mayor took up a position on the floor immediately in front of me. The crowd passed on down the hall to the pile of rubbish in the rear. But their leader, seeing that this was not just the thing, turned about as I had expected and led the others back to the workbench. He was at once made chairman of the meeting; I think I made the motion. When he was voted in, he was on the floor at the end of the bench. The mayor, as I have said, was on the floor before me, while I was standing on the bench overlooking all.

The moment the chairman was elected, and before anyone else could speak, I addressed him and was recognized. By this I gained the chance to make the first speech—both advantages of great importance in the circumstances. All this time, although I had given them no reason so to believe, the crowd thought I was in sympathy with them. Without losing any time, however, I proceeded to let them know how I stood. For three or four minutes, in the most passionate words I could utter, I denounced the purpose of those who had called the meeting. I pointed out the absence of the slightest need for us to imbrue our hands in the blood of a prisoner who so soon would be tried and executed under the forms of the law. I also pointed out how difficult it would be to take the prisoner out of the custody of a man like Dave Cook, one of the most nervy sheriffs who had ever held office. Knowing that it was his duty, he would shoot before giving up his prisoner.

With this, I reminded the meeting, for the second time, that it was the duty of others to punish the guilty men, not ours, and that if we killed the prisoner by mob violence, we would all be guilty of base cowardice and murder. Without pausing, I then moved that the meeting should adjourn. This was loudly seconded by the mayor, and I called upon the chairman to put the question to vote. The latter, looking from me to the mayor, after a little hesitation put the question. The motion carried and the crowd dispersed. A crowd of men, frantic with fear or anger, is much like a herd of stampeded cattle. The thing is to get in the lead of the mob and divert the attention of its unreasoning, maddened members—just as a knowing cowboy, when possible, rides in the lead of the stampeded herd and leads them around in a circle until the danger is past.[72]

CHAPTER FOURTEEN

Deadwood Lawyer 1874-1877

IN 1874, after five years service as postmaster of Denver, I was removed by President Grant. This was a result of a controversy over the appointment of S. H. Elbert as governor of the territory against the application of Edward M. McCook, who was seeking reappointment.[73] Certain parties took advantage of the political situation to charge me with mismanagement of the mails. The removal—or rather, my resignation, from the office—caused me more loss than the salary.[74] For owing to the very great increase in the mails, I had bought several more stacks of letter boxes. These my successor in the office refused to buy from me at any price, and I could not sell or use them elsewhere. Before long the charges against me were proved utterly false, as were the false charges by the same parties against David G. Moffat regarding public lands. When, later on, my successor as postmaster was removed, the position was tendered to me. I declined in favor of my former assistant, Edward Summer, who received the appointment.

Meantime I had devoted all my time to my law practice. But in 1876, when Colorado was admitted as a state, the privilege was given me to take part in organizing the state government.[75] I was elected on the Republican ticket as a state senator, and served during the first session of the state legislature.[76] One measure I proposed and had passed—as a precaution against loss of life from fire or panic—was an act requiring the doors of all public buildings to open outwards.

Late in the fall of 1876, the year of Custer's battle and death at the Little Big Horn River, a Jew of Deadwood, Dakota Territory, had come to Denver and purchased bills of goods from several of our merchants. These included dry goods from Daniels and Fisher and J. K. Doolittle, hardware from George Tritch, and clothing from A. Jacobs and Company. He paid only a small amount of cash down, and shipped the goods off to Deadwood under promise that he would sell them rapidly and remit the balance he owed on them in two or three months. The goods went to Deadwood all right. But instead of being put up for sale at retail, the Denver creditors learned that all the goods were stored in hiding. Such was the status of the business in the spring of 1877, when the creditors put their claims into my hands and advanced money for me to proceed to Deadwood. There I was to make collection of the full amount due them, or else to make a compromise, if the law in the mining camp was not adequate.

So it was that on April 9, 1877, I packed my trunk and started for Deadwood. Fellow travelers were George W. Brown and William H. Claggett. The former told me that he had $12,000 in bills on his person, inside the lining of his clothes. He intended to go [into] banking with the money at Deadwood as Brown and Shum. Claggett intended to open a law office in Deadwood. I had known Brown many years but Claggett only for a few months. He was a mining lawyer from the western states—lastly, I think from Montana.

We went by rail to Cheyenne and put up for the night at B. L. Ford's hotel. The next morning, after an early breakfast, we left town in the coach for Deadwood, said to be three hundred miles away. It was a good Concord coach, and its team of four fine American horses took us and two other passengers due north over the rolling prairie on a good road at the regular stage gait of six miles an hour. It was a nice ride and we congratulated ourselves that the trip to Deadwood would not be so fatiguing as we had thought.

Before we left Denver, we knew that our journey would be accomplished by more or less danger from attacks by holdups and possibly by Indians while crossing the Badlands. And all six of us, counting the driver, were armed and would be on the alert for any danger that might arise. So we had not been restrained from making the trip by the thought of danger. George Brown, however, owing to carrying so much money on his person, was not wholly unconcerned. He did not fear so much for his life as for the loss of his money if the coach should be held up by highwaymen. He had "sand," and I think he would have risked being killed to save his money.

So we rolled along away from Cheyenne in high spirits. But, sad to relate, at the first stage station we had to change from the comfortable coach and team of big American horses to a lumber wagon drawn by four smaller animals. The driver and one of the strangers occupied the spring seat, the only one on the wagon. The rest of us had to sit on the trunks and baggage. I was perched with the other stranger on the swell top of a Saratoga trunk.[77] This was at the back of the wagon, where we had all the jar of the back axle. We sat a few inches above the wagon bed with nothing for us to rest against to prevent a fall overboard backwards. Nor was it any better on each side. The trunk being highest in the middle, our seats sloped to the outer ends, without anything to brace us. This was bad enough on level road. On sliding ground, especially where rough and rocky, we had to tense our muscles to keep from being pitched out of the wagon over the hind wheels. I have traveled a great deal in my life by stage and wagon, and I am free to say I never had a harder or more dangerous ride than all the rest of the trip, two hundred and more miles, to Deadwood.

We had no more than been seated, and the wagon going at six miles an hour, than I knew what I was up against. All the time there was the "spring" of the hind axle, and all the time the danger of slipping over sideways or back over the tailboard. Very thankful we were when we reached the Home station at the crossing of Chugwater Creek and stopped for supper. Mrs. Tom Smith, the landlady, I had known years before in Denver. Seated at the table on a cane-seat chair, I enjoyed very much the good meal and her cheerful conversation. The chair was level and had a back. All too soon, right after supper, the cry was "All aboard!" and we had to return to our seats on the wagon-stage. We traveled all night. I could not say how many stations we passed. I "rested" in a heap between my own trunk and the seat ahead, with my feet and overshoes under me and my overcoat and hat my only covering. I had no dreams nor enough bits of sleep to have floated a dream.

At noon the next day we passed Fort Laramie and reached Hat Creek that night after dark. On coming out from supper I found the public room full of people, among them a platoon of U.S. soldiers. There was much loud talk that sounded and smelled as if inspired by bad whiskey. In front of me, as I stepped inside, stood a soldier with a dagger in his hand behind his back. It looked as if he intended to use the blade on someone in the room. I sidestepped the soldier and hastily pushed my way to the outer door. The stage was about ready to leave. As I hurriedly took my place aboard, I asked the driver what the row was about in the barroom. He said a guard of soldiers had come from the nearby military post to arrest a drunken soldier who was raising Cain with the civilians.

That night we entered the Badlands. While still in them, the next noon, we stopped to change teams at a desolate stage station "garrisoned" by only one man. While we waited, three Indians came in sight about a quarter of a mile away to the left of the road. Claggett had got his rifle to shoot a crow perched on a cottonwood tree some two hundred yards away. When we first saw the Indians, they were standing still, hesitating, I thought, whether to come on or retreat. I was nervous, for this was less than a year after Custer's defeat on the Little Big Horn River, not over a hundred and fifty miles from this stage station. Many Indians were still hostile and on the warpath.

But Claggett did not seem alarmed. He stood forward, raised his rifle, and fired. Down fell the crow. It was a splendid shot at so great a distance. Best of all, it proved to the Indians that we were well armed and knew how to shoot. They came peacefully towards us and begged some "tobac," keeping their weapons, if they had any, out of sight under their blankets.

The stock tender said he was glad it happened our being there, as he had no faith in Indians. In this he voiced the sentiments of our entire party. At such a time and place on the *Bad*lands, any Indians were all too likely to be *bad*. However, the unwelcome callers did not linger long. Soon after they left we also went our way, leaving the lonely stock tender in dread that the Indians would return. I would not have taken his place for all the wealth of the Black Hills, without more weapons of defense than he had in his dugout.

By noon we left the Badlands and came in sight of the Black Hills. For miles and miles ahead they made a black line all along the horizon. As we neared where they rose above the general level of the plain, we saw they were covered with a thick growth of evergreen trees. Our road passed into the hills and entered a rocky red canyon. Here the driver pointed out the graves of three prospectors who had been killed and scalped by Indians the fall before. Three or four miles farther on we came to a military company in camp under the pines, a most beautiful spot for a picnic. How delighted I was to reach the first and only place since leaving Cheyenne where I felt a sense of security. For a few minutes we called on the officer in command. He was as glad to see us as we were to see him and his soldiers. He left with "smiles" to him and his adjutant.

By evening we reached Custer, the county seat of Custer County. There we put up at the Custer House for the night. It was the only hotel in the place, quite a good frame building, painted white. The town could not be called large. We were able to look it over at a glance owing to the fewness of houses to obstruct the view. The next morning, bright and early, we set out for Deadwood, determined to reach it by night.

After passing the military camp the day before, we had no fear of Indians. But, oh, the rain and mud that we encountered that last day of our journey! The road from Custer was through the woods all the way, in mud uphill and down except when out of it on "corduroy"— the cross-laid pavement of logs.

In the afternoon we passed the place where our driver told us the coach had been attacked by highwaymen about two weeks before. The robbers had killed the driver, Johnny Stantiler, and stole from the coach five or six thousand dollars worth of Deadwood placer gold. The account of this holdup made George Brown more nervous than ever over the chance of losing his $13,000 in paper money. He would not sit quiet, but would jump off and walk beside the stage every little while, then jump on again. All the time he kept peering around every crook and turn of the road for "road agents" waiting to get his money. I had no such fear of any attack because it was the outgoing stages carrying gold dust and nuggets that were held up by white robbers. I said so to George, but nothing would calm him until we reached Deadwood.

When we came to the end of our journey, we were not only wet to the skin; horses, stage, baggage, and passengers and all were covered with mud. In this condition we drove up to a small two-story building on Main Street that bore the name of Grand Central Hotel. It was kept by Wagner, a thrifty Dutchman.

We had arrived at dusk. There was quite a lot of people standing in front of the hotel to receive us. As we came to a stop, a stentorian voice called: "Is Colonel Claggett, the silver-tongued orator from Montana, on this coach?" Being assured that he was, the same voice started cheering for Claggett. I went across the street and registered at the Custer House, run by an American. It was a new board building, quite open and exposed to the weather. That night and every other night that I kept the room and bed there, I slept in damp sheets. The outer wall of my room was made of green lumber of single thickness. The boards had shrunk, opening cracks in the wall that let in the dampness from the rain and soft snow that beat against the side of the house. This Custer House was the biggest and best hotel in Deadwood. But owing to the conditions I have mentioned, I contracted a throat trouble that gave my voice a huskiness that has never left me. The hotel food was poor yet the best the market afforded. They served the same thing over and over three times a day on a red linen tablecloth.

Though I at once set about looking after the business I had come on, I made little progress on it. Meantime I hustled around to find a better room and bed. After three weeks I succeeded in getting a Mr. McCuchen to build me a shack of boards on his back lot. He excavated the site out of a snowbank. This "shebang" was made all of green lumber—walls, partition, doors, and windows. But the boards were closely nailed together. They kept out the rain and snow. I bought a box stove, about two feet long, and five joints of stove pipe. Set up in the front room, this cost me twenty-six dollars. In Denver the same would have been dear at four dollars. My bed was a springless lounge with only a canvas, a buffalo robe, a pair of blankets, and my over-coat for bedding. By keeping my stove hot with pitch-pine fuel from early morning until I retired to bed at midnight, I dried out and was warm and comfortable day and night. After getting a chair, a table, some stationery, and a copy of the codes of Dakota, I chalked "Law Office" on the outside of my door.

All the time that I was getting myself so elegantly settled I was keep-ing a lookout for the "lame dust" I had come to capture. Though I had appointments with him to talk over the matter, he would give me no satisfaction whatever, nor could I learn from him or from anyone else where the goods were hidden. I could find nothing to attach. Matters stood thus for weeks, with nothing done and nothing doing to make the collection of his debts. Meanwhile I met some old Nebraska friends who were at Deadwood in the mining business. They needed advice and counsel, and paid me a good retainer. I so managed their business that it was settled to their entire satisfaction without having to go to court. For this they paid me well.

About the middle of May, Ben Holstein, who knew why I was in camp, said to me that my man would give forty cents on the dollar in full payment of the claims I held against him. I at once declined the offer. But Ben said I had better take it. On further inquiries among other friends in Deadwood, I began to think more favorably of the compromise. When I wrote the facts to my Denver clients, all of them promptly authorized me to accept the forty cents on the dollar offer. This I did and remitted to each creditor his share, retaining a reasonable fee for the collection.

During this transaction, more and more business came into my office. That encouraged me to think of remaining in Deadwood a year or more during the mining boom. I sent to Denver for a few of my law books. Then, early in July, I bought a large log house on the hillside street above and parallel with Main Street. It was reached by sixty or eighty steps of a board stairway. Having now a house for my family, I sent money for them to join me.

My wife at once packed up our household goods and shipped them by wagon freight to Deadwood. Then, with all the children, she came north by stage. Fortunately, unlike my experience, their conveyance was a regular coach, not a wagon. Yet the trip was very hard and fatiguing for a mother with five children, the youngest a little girl only four years old. The stage was due in Deadwood at nightfall but did not get in until the next morning, July 12. All night long I waited and listened for the rattle of the coach, unable to sleep. That last night my wife also had been unable to sleep. She had been kept awake by her fear of stage robbers. But the children had slept well, the younger two lolling on their mother's lap.

We camped in our house on the hillside until the household goods arrived by the slow wagon freight. After that, with them, we had a comfortable furnished home in the big log cabin. I changed my law office to a better room in a building built on the hillside halfway up the stairway from Main Street. Claggett and W. C. Kingsley had their law office in the same building. My practice brought me in enough money to pay all current expenses.

After we were settled and my wife was rested, she seemed well satisfied to live in a mining camp with her husband and children, as long as it was to my best interests to remain. Our children enjoyed being there more than ourselves. They could play among the pines on the hill above our cabin, also up City Creek, or across town at the White Rocks.

We did not feel the same. For one thing, the town was in some respects too much like Denver in the early days—wide-open drinking and gambling, many fights, and not infrequent killings. Only the previous year Wild Bill (James Butler) Hickok, a fine frontiersman and the greatest of law-enforcing gunfighters, had been assassinated by a badman named McCoy. No less unpleasant were the attacks by Indians on white men in the country all around the Black Hills. Only a month or two before I reached Deadwood, a small war party had fired down the mountain into the town. When they were pursued, an Indian who had been wounded, in turn mortally wounded a pioneer preacher named Smith. Now and then, all during 1877, other war parties attacked travelers, sometimes killing and scalping a man or two.

CHAPTER FIFTEEN

Later Years 1878-1914

IN THE SPRING of 1878, illness of Robert, my youngest son, caused me to take my family back to Denver. We left Deadwood by way of the stage route south through Buffalo Gap for Sidney, Nebraska. We had a meal at a stage station out on the plains beyond the Hills. A few hours after we left the place, it was struck by a war party. All persons there, men and women alike, were killed and scalped; some were tortured. This we learned before changing from coach to train at Sidney.

Back in Denver, I rented a cottage between Thirteenth and Fourteenth avenues on Broadway across from the old Broadway School. Leaving my wife and children well housed, I at once went westwards over the mountains and opened a law office at the booming silver mining camp of Leadville. The next year I became right-of-way attorney for the Denver and Rio Grande Railroad. Rails were being laid at that time from Fairplay to Alma. From that town a coach stage line climbed Mosquito Pass to Leadville. The Denver and Rio Grande reached the big camp in July 1880, thence headed on westwards for Rock Creek.

During 1880, in association with Isaac Cooper and others, we laid out the town of Aspen. Later on, Cooper and myself, together with John Blake, William Gilder, and Frank Erizensperger, formed the Defiance Town and Land Company. Our purpose was to promote the present Glenwood Springs district as a health resort. The now famous medicinal hot springs there had been used by the Ute Indians to cure sickness ages before the coming of the white man. The townsite, near where the Roaring Fork falls into the Colorado River (then called the Grand), was named Defiance. But in 1883 we changed it to Glenwood Springs, after Glenwood, Iowa, where I had first practiced law in 1851-1854.[78]

During the mid-eighties an idea occurred to me how to benefit Colorado. As should be well known, nearly all land in the West belonged to the federal government except what was granted to homesteaders and railroads and to Indians on reservations. Upon the admission of Colorado to statehood in 1876 the government had donated to it, for school purposes, sections 16 and 32 in each township of the public lands.[79] This grant, however, included no sections on the Ute Indian reservation, which then covered a vast area in western Colorado, larger than some eastern states and which by treaty belonged to the Utes. Considering this great loss to the school fund of Colorado, I thought out a plan for obtaining compensation. When I explained my idea to state senator George M. Chilcott, he had the legislature pass a bill that created the position of state agent, March 31, 1885.

[On] April 2, 1885, I was appointed such state agent by Governor Eaton and at once undertook to obtain from the federal government school lands in lieu of those that would have been granted to Colorado on the Ute Indian reservation if there had been no reservation.[80] My appointment did not provide for any expenses or salary. My only pay, if any, depended upon the contingency that I should gain such grant of school lands. In that case, I was to be paid at the rate of six and a quarter cents an acre of the lands recovered—that is, five per cent of the value of the lands at $1.25 per acre.

The matter was first presented to the U. S. Land Office at Glenwood Springs, Colorado. There after months of delay, the following September, 1885, it at last met with an adverse decision. I then went on to Washington and in January 1886 appealed to the commissioner of the General Land Office, presenting a brief for a reversal of the unfavorable decision. Despite my arguments and attempts to obtain action, the case was held up a whole year, until January 29, 1887. Then, finally, the commissioner confirmed the adverse decision. Thereupon I appealed to the secretary of the interior, who, after months more of arguments and other efforts by me, nearly a year later, December 6, 1887, overruled the commissioner and decided that Colorado was entitled to the school lands in lieu of those lost on the Ute reservation.

But this did not settle the matter. It next had to be passed upon by Congress. I drew up a bill (which was introduced in the Senate by Senator Teller) authorizing the state of Colorado to select such indemnity school lands. As a former delegate from Colorado, I was entitled to the privilege of the floor, hence was able to talk with senators and representatives explaining the purpose of the bill and urging its passage. These efforts, together with those of our congressmen, succeeded after much difficulty in getting the bill through the committees, then winning a favorable vote from both houses, and finally the signature of the president.

All that, however, far from ended my work. Upon returning to Denver, I had to urge the commissioners of the State Land Board to select sections of the newly granted school lands. Naturally they were in no hurry to do so. Unlike myself they were not in need of being paid for years of service. When lists of selections were at last made up, I had to take them to Washington for approval by the U. S. Land Office. There followed more tedious delay and work. The officials were not only indifferent, they had to be convinced that the law really gave Colorado the right to the lands selected. To get an approval of that list, I had to employ at stiff pay a regular Federal Land Office attorney who knew the ropes and how to obtain results from bureaucrats.

Finally, after all the months and years of my work, expenses, and waiting, I brought back to Denver the approved lists. Having earned my six and a quarter cents an acre for the many sections of school lands now in possession of the state, I applied for the payment due me. The legislature that created a state agent passed a standing appropriation out of which to pay the agent's compensation, if and when earned. But now the state treasurer held that this appropriation was in the *third class* and there was only enough money in the treasury to pay *state officers* who belonged to the *first class.* This compelled me to take the matter to the courts. When it was tried, the district court held that *I* was a *state officer.* The attorney general appealed. But the supreme court confirmed the decision in my favor. Then, at long last, I received my hard-earned pay.

But owing to the years of delay and to my heavy expenses and loss of other law practice, I had been [un]able to pay off the mortgage on my home on Acoma Street near Colfax Avenue. The property was lost to me at foreclosure of the mortgage not a great while before the city of Denver bought it and all other properties in the proposed Civic Center at very good prices.

The school lands were not all that I won for Colorado as state agent. In 1890 I also obtained $60,864 for the state, being five percent of the money the federal government had received from the sale of public lands since 1876. My pay for this was $3,043. There was other business I did for the state.

In March 1897 ill health and the old pioneer urge caused me to move to the new town of Port Arthur, Texas. There, shortly afterwards, I lost my beloved wife, Clara Ames Bennet. Next came a hurricane and then stagnation of the town due to litigation that tied up all construction on the projected ship canal up to there from the Gulf of Mexico at Sabine Pass. There being no law practice in town for me, I returned to Denver where I opened an office, sharing that of my old friend Louis Dugal.[81]

After that, months and years passed while smaller lists of school land selections were made up and put through the mill of bureaucracy. Unable to stand the loss of time and expense of going to Washington, I had to allow a third of my compensation to the Federal Land Office attorney, C. C. Clements, to push the lists through the General Land Office. Also in 1900 a new treasurer and attorney general would not allow me my pay until I had again won a decision in my favor from the courts. In 1908, when I was eighty-two years old, and twenty-three years after I became state agent, lists were approved that entitled me to something over $2,000. But the standing appropriation had been used up. To pay me, a bill was introduced in the then legislature entitled "For the Relief of Hiram P. Bennet." This looked as if I were asking for charity, not for what was due me. But such is the form of like bills.

As usual, appropriations are hard to get passed unless they have strong political backing. Having none, the best I could do was personally to ask the legislators for a favorable consideration of my case.[82] With this purpose in mind, I started to go over town to the State Capitol. But when stepping from a street car, a sudden jerk by it flung me off and down. The fall upon the concrete street pavement broke my right hip. If the police ambulance that was summoned had taken me to a hospital, I would not have survived the shock of my injury. Even at home, with the best of medical and surgical attention, I would have died but for the care and nursing of Susan, the wife of Robert, my youngest son. In the past years, she had already brought me through two very serious illnesses.

While I lay hovering between life and death, Hiram, my oldest son, represented me before the legislature. After much hemming and hawing, the lawmakers at last graciously agreed to appropriate enough to pay what was due me—provided I signed away all claim to any future compensation that might accrue to me as state agent. To do this I could do no other than consent in view of my heavy medical and surgical bills. In the long run, the six and a quarter cents an acre I received during those many years was small requital for all my work, expenses, loss of my regular law practice, and my worry over the many delays—to say nothing of the fact that I alone was the person who conceived the idea and plan to obtain those school lands in lieu of the ones lost on the Ute and other reservations. All those thousands of sections won by me for the state were, as regards my compensation, valued at only $1.25 an acre. Yet they really were worth at least $5 an acre, and many of them were much more valuable. However, I am content that I obtained for my state over 660,000 acres of land that would not otherwise have come into the ownership of the school fund.

After a long convalescence, I at last partially recovered from my injury. But there was no bony union of my broken hip. I have never since been able to walk without crutches. Otherwise I have enjoyed good health. Though unable to resume law practice, my disability has not prevented me from visiting my son John, and the family of Sara, my oldest daughter, in Montana, and of Blanche, my youngest daughter, at Greeley and Estes Park, as well as the family of my oldest son, Hiram, across town. This and living with Robert and Susan and their son Harold at our home has made the six years since my injury the happiest of my life. Now, at my eighty-eighth birthday, September 2, 1914, I am keenly alert to the beginnings of the great war in Europe.

BIOGRAPHICAL NOTE

After a brief illness, Hiram Pitt Bennet departed this life November 11, seventy days after his birthday. To the very last, his mind remained no less clear and active than throughout his long life. Other than finishing his memoirs, he had thought only for the present and future. He kept track of world events and was interested in sociology, politics, and certain aspects of religion.

1

This carbon copy, now in the possession of the Colorado Historical Society, contains additional marks in blue pen made by Charlotte Waters, Bennet's great-granddaughter, sometime before it was submitted for publication. These consist of editorial changes in punctuation and the insertion of chapter divisions. We have kept the chapter divisions as they stand and have added chapter titles in the printed version.

Further changes in punctuation and organization of paragraphs deserves some comment. Since the memoirs were not written in Hiram Bennet's own hand but dictated to his son Robert, who presumably prepared the typescript, we have not felt bound in this case to the well-established principle of reprinting historical manuscripts verbatim. Furthermore, at certain points in the typescript it is clear that Robert "improved" upon his father's natural speech patterns. The extent of this editorial license is unknown and, given the general flow of the narrative, probably minor. But it is unlikely that Hiram Bennet would have made the following laborious statement, drawn from the text: "Grain was reaped with cradle-scythes, to swing which, according to jokers, a man required a strong back and a weak head."

Thus, since the conventions of paragraphing, punctuation, spelling, and capitalization are those of the transcriber, not Bennet himself, it is our feeling that nothing of historical value would be lost, and much gained, by making a few editorial changes for the sake of readability. This does not apply to sentence structure, grammar, or substantive matters of style, which have not been altered.

2

The sons of Elisha and Maria Bradbury Bennet were, in the order of their birth: Isiah, John, Elisha, Hiram, Thomas, Joseph, William, and David (who died at birth).

3

Bennet's parents moved in September possibly because that month allowed them to get their crops in, which provided them with extra money as well as supplies for their journeys. Also, moving westward as they did permitted them a month to six weeks of reasonably good weather in which to travel. Note that this was the month in which they made other moves and in which Hiram Bennet and his brother departed for the Pikes Peak gold fields in 1859.

4

Thomas L. Karnes, *William Gilpin: Western Nationalist* (Austin: University of Texas Press, 1970), 257.

5

Stephen F. Nuckolls also moved to Colorado and became a well-known merchant and entrepreneur in the Central City and Georgetown areas. In 1863 he went to New York where he organized several mining companies (*Georgetown Courier,* March 27, 1884, p. 3). These firms doubtless were part of the speculation boom in Colorado mines that occurred in 1863 and early 1864. Bennet was connected with him in several of these ventures (*Daily Mining Journal* [Black Hawk], June 12, 1865, p. 3).

6

Bennet's name figures prominently in many of the early land transactions in Glenwood Springs. One has only to leaf through the early grantor-grantee indices in the office of the Garfield County Clerk and Recorder in Grand Junction to verify his activities. See also Lena M. Urquhart, *Glenwood Springs: Spa in the Mountains* (Boulder: Pruett Publishing Co., 1970), 34, 38–39, which tells of Bennet's connection with early Glenwood Springs.

7

Jerome C. Smiley, *History of Denver* (1901; reprint ed., Evansville, Ind.: Unigraphic, Inc., 1971), 782.

8
Lyle Dorsett, *The Queen City: A History of Denver* (Boulder: Pruett Publishing Co., 1977), 8-12.

9
Jonas H. Oakes must have been the father of another noted Colorado pioneer, Maj. D. C. Oakes. See Wilbur Fiske Stone, *History of Colorado*, 4 vols. (Chicago: S. J. Clarke Publishing Co., 1918), 2:614-16.

10
Doubtless Bennet is referring to Oliver Hazard Perry's decisive victory against the British at the Battle of Lake Erie.

11
Chesterville lies west of Waterville and southeast of Farmington, Maine, just a little to the south of the state's center. The Bennet family chose a southwesterly course as they crossed the Androscoggin River in Maine, the White Mountains in New Hampshire, and the Green Mountains in Vermont before reaching the Hudson and then Saratoga Springs, New York. From Saratoga Springs they went almost due west to Utica, where they loaded their wagons on the Erie Canal boat which took them across western New York to Lockport.

When they chose the Erie Canal, the Bennets joined many of the contemporary New Englanders who sought better farmland in the West, although Elisha Bennet was among those still moving to Ohio. The canal, while crowded, provided its users with cheap and dependable transportation; however, it did divert the main course of travel from Ohio to the new lands in Michigan, Indiana, and Illinois. See Ray A. Billington, *Westward Expansion: A History of the American Frontier*, 3d ed. (New York: Macmillan Co., 1967), 301.

Upon leaving the canal, the Bennets would have rumbled along to the east of Niagara Falls and followed a track on the east side of Lake Erie, through Erie, Pennsylvania, into Cleveland, Ohio. Finally, they headed southwest from Cleveland to

Galion, some eight miles west of present-day Mansfield, Ohio.

12
Buckwheat, character, and *patent* were terms applied to shaped-note musical notation in which the shape of the note denoted its relation to singing syllables (e.g., do, re, me). See Stanley Sadne, ed., *The New Grove Dictionary of Music and Musicians*, 3d ed., 20 vols. (London: Macmillan Publishers, 1980), 17:223-28.

13
Joseph Robidoux established a trading post on the Missouri River near Blacksnake Hills in northwestern Missouri for the American Fur Company in 1826. At that time his log house was the only building on the site of present-day St. Joseph. See *History of Buchanan County, Missouri* (St. Joseph, Mo.: Union Historical Co., 1881), 394-95.

14
The Bennet family route took them from Galion through Delaware, Worthington, and Dayton in Ohio; Richmond, Indianapolis, and Terre Haute in Indiana; Vandalia and Alton in Illinois; and then Richmond, Liberty, and finally Savannah, Missouri, some twenty to twenty-five miles north of St. Joseph.

15
Contemporary maps, including the *Map of the State of Iowa* (Philadelphia: Thomas Cowperthwaite & Co., 1850), show "Huntsacker's Ferry"; L. Lingenfelter (*History of Fremont County, Iowa* [1881; reprint ed.; Evansville, Ind.: Unigraphic, Inc., 1975], 373) mentions Isaac "Hunsaker" as one of Fremont County's first commissioners and tells of "Hunsacker's" arrival in the 1840s.

16
Trader's Point was located on the east bank of the Missouri River across from present-day Bellevue, Nebraska. See *A Township Map of the State of Iowa* (Fairfield, Iowa: Henn, Williams & Co. and Philadelphia: R. L. Barnes, 1855).

17

Allen A. Bradford, like Bennet, was a Maine native who spent his young adulthood on the edge of the frontier in northwestern Missouri and later moved to Colorado. See *Biographical Directory of the American Congress, 1774–1971* (Washington, D.C.: Government Printing Office, 1971), 624–25.

18

E. H. Cowles, in his reminiscences, includes Bennet at a convention urging negotiations with the Indians in the winter of 1853–54 but places the meeting in St. Joseph. See "Otoe County in Early Days, by E. H. Cowles, One of the Oldest Settlers," *Transactions and Reports of the Nebraska State Historical Society* (Lincoln: State Journal Co., 1885), 1:39.

19

In fact, Bennet was one of the organizers of Bellevue in early 1854. He joined Col. Peter A. Sarpy and others as original proprietors of the Old Town Company. See S. D. Bangs, "History of Sarpy County," *Transactions and Reports of the Nebraska State Historical Society*, 2:295.

20

"H. P. Bennet, active, impulsive, a ready off-hand speaker, commanded the respect of his colleagues and the good will of all members of the council. He was of medium stature, light hair, his complexion varying from pale to florid to fit the state of his varying intensity of feeling in debate. He was pleasant, sociable, and affable with his associates. He was a strong worker for south of the Platte and for the best interests of his constituents" (Samuel E. Rogers, "Sketches of Members of the Legislature of 1855," *Proceedings and Collections of the Nebraska State Historical Society*, 2d ser., vol. 2 [Lincoln: State Journal Co., 1898], 117–18).

21

Probably Lafayette Nuckolls, younger brother of Stephen F. and Columbus ("Lum") Nuckolls.

22

Joseph Sharp is described as instrumental in the matter of the capital's removal but leaving the legislature "as empty-handed as when he entered it." See J. Sterling Morton, ed., *Illustrated History of Nebraska* (Lincoln: Jacob North & Co., 1907), 1:196n, 198–99.

23

Oliver Wendell Holmes's *Autocrat at the Breakfast Table* was published initially as a set of highly witty and popular essays serialized from 1857 to 1858 in the *Atlantic Monthly*, edited by his friend James Russell Lowell. See Robert Spiller et al., *Literary History of the United States: History*, 3d ed. rev. (New York and London: Macmillan Co., 1963), 599–600.

24

Stephen Friel Nuckolls (1825–79) was a founder of Nebraska City. A merchant, banker, and railroad man, he served in the territorial legislature and may have been a slaveholder. His entrepreneurship was carried on in Missouri, Iowa, Nebraska, Wyoming, and Utah. See *Biographical Directory of Congress*, 1479, and Rev. John Todd, *Early Settlement and Growth of Western Iowa, or Reminiscences* (Des Moines: Historical Department of Iowa, 1906), 141–42.

25

Bird Beers Chapman (1821–71) was described as a "Bird of passage," a temporary resident of Nebraska. See Thomas Weston Tipton, "Forty Years of Nebraska at Home and in Congress," in *Proceedings and Collections of the Nebraska State Historical Society*, 2d ser., vol. 4 (Lincoln: State Journal Co., 1902), 81.

26

Napoleon Bonaparte Giddings (1816–97) served briefly (January 5 to March 4, 1855) as territorial delegate from Nebraska. See *Biographical Directory of Congress*, 999.

27
Contesting elections was a common practice at this time. During the Thirty-fourth Congress there were eight such cases in the House. See D. W. Bartlett, comp., *Cases of Contested Elections in Congress from 1834 to 1865*, Misc. Doc. No. 57 (Washington, D.C.: Government Printing Office, 1865), 647.

28
James Wilson Grimes (1816–72) served as governor of Iowa between 1854 and 1858 and was elected senator from Iowa in 1859. See *Biographical Directory of Congress*, 1036.

29
Possibly John Jordan Crittenden, senator (1855–61) from Kentucky. See *Biographical Directory of Congress*, 802.

30
Later in the manuscript Bennet states, "At that time the Senate sat in what is now the Supreme Court room, and the House in what is now known as Statuary or Monument Hall." This sentence has now been removed from the text, where it originally appeared out of context.

31
The final vote actually took place on February 2, 1856. See *Congressional Globe*, House, 34th Cong., 1st sess., February 2, 1856, 337.

32
For an account of Nathaniel P. Banks, see *Biographical Directory of Congress*, 549.

33
Banks was escorted by a committee of three: Lewis Davis Campbell, William Mills Fuller, and William Aiken. While Howell Cobb was a representative in the House at that time, he was not a part of the escort group. See *Congressional Globe*, House, 34th Cong., 1st sess., February 2, 1856, 342.

34
This was the Thirty-fourth Congress.

35
The vote and absence of pay are confirmed in Fred Harvey Harrington, "The First Northern Victory," *Journal of Southern History* 5 (May 1939): 197.

36
The Election Committee report presented by Watson on April 18 recommended that Bennet be seated. It was not until May 13 that Stephens presented the committee's minority report, which contained information from J. L. Sharp and was in favor of seating Chapman. The final vote was held on July 22. See *Cases of Contested Elections*, 204–14.

37
No Solomon G. Davis served in the Thirty-fourth—or any—Congress, but there was a Solomon G. Haven in the Thirty-fourth Congress (*Biographical Directory of Congress*, 1088).

38
The final vote was sixty-three yeas and sixty-nine nays on the resolution "That Bird B. Chapman is not entitled to a seat in this body as a Delegate from the Territory of Nebraska," so Bennet lost by six votes. Neither Davis nor Carlile appears in the roll call, while Haven is listed as voting "yea" (*Congressional Globe*, House, 34th Cong., 1st sess., July 22, 1856, 1729).

39
Mileage and per diem were approved, although the amount was not specified (*Congressional Globe*, House, 34th Cong., 1st sess., July 22, 1856, 1729).

40
The Greeley-Rust incident developed as a result of the long Speaker contest. "After a hundred ballots had failed, Rust vainly offered a resolution suggesting that the names of the contending candidates be withdrawn; and that recommendation a *Tribune* editorial branded . . . a 'discreditable proposition.' Rust took offense and sought out Greeley. . . . twice he set upon the editor, first on the Capitol

grounds and later at a hotel. In neither in-
stance did Greeley make any attempt to
defend himself" (Granville D. Davis,
"Arkansas and the Blood of Kansas,"
Journal of Southern History 16
(November 1950): 445-46.

41
Brooks was not expelled from the House.
The special committee reported in favor
of expulsion but the report failed to
receive the two-thirds majority needed to
pass. Brooks then resigned from Congress but was reelected to fill his own
vacancy and served until his death in
1857. See *Dictionary of American
Biography* 3:88 and *Congressional
Globe*, appendix, House, 34th Cong., 1st
sess., July 14, 1856, 831-33.

42
On the contrary, Brooks, who died
relatively soon after the attack, never expressed regret for his assault on Sumner.
His letter to the House on May 29, 1856,
states that the assault "made in the Senate
Chamber was caused only by the fact
that, after a careful search elsewhere, on
the previous as well as on the same day,
the offender [Sumner] could not be found
outside the walls of the Senate Chamber."
His actions were carefully considered,
and at least immediately following the incident he seemed to have no doubts about
his attack. His resignation speech is
similarly clear: "I went to work very
deliberately, as I am charged—and this is
admitted—and speculated somewhat as
to whether I should employ a whip or a
cowhide" (*Congressional Globe*, Senate,
34th Cong., 1st and 2d sess., 1347, and
House, appendix, 34th Cong., 1st sess.,
July 14, 1856, 832.

43
The Platte Valley Bank was owned by
Stephen F. Nuckolls. See Henry W. Yates,
"Early Nebraska Currency and Per
Capita Circulation," *Proceedings of the
Nebraska State Historical Society* 1 (Oc-
tober 1894): 71.

44
Bennet and his party, with shotguns,
resembled the argonauts of 1859, most of
whom arrived in Denver armed with at
least one rifle and shotgun. See Frank
Hall, *History of the State of Colorado*, 4
vols. (Chicago: Blakely Printing Co.,
1889-95), 1:271.

45
Jim Baker had a cabin on Clear Creek
near "where the then stage road crossed
the creek," and his toll bridge was
established by the time Bennet moved to
Denver. See Chauncey Thomas, "Some
Characteristics of Jim Baker," *The Colorado Magazine* 4 (August 1927):
142-43, and Percy Stanley Fritz, *Colorado: Centennial State* (New York:
Prentice-Hall, Inc., 1941), 90.

46
Bennet and D. C. Oakes were cousins and
must have been boyhood friends,
although Oakes was a little more than a
year older. Oakes was born in Carthage,
Maine, on April 3, 1826. In 1831 he
moved with his parents to Galion, Ohio,
where his mother died the following year.
After her death, his father moved the
family to Lagrange County, Indiana, and
then to Clinton County, Iowa. In 1849 the
twenty-four-year-old Oakes and two
others sought their fortunes unsuccessful-
ly in California. Oakes returned to Iowa,
where he married Olive Maria Martin
and moved to Glenwood, Iowa, to
become a builder and contractor.
During fall 1858 Oakes visited the gold
fields located in western Kansas and
Nebraska, returning to Iowa full of enthusiasm for the area's prospects. He then
wrote and published *Pike's Peak Guide
and Journal*, for which he was roundly
criticized by many argonauts in 1859. He
was back in what became Colorado in the
spring of 1859 bringing with him a
sawmill that he operated on Plum Creek
thirty miles south of Denver until he sold
it in 1865. That year President Andrew
Johnson appointed him agent for several
bands of Utes, the first Indian agency
established for the Mountain Utes. In

October 1869 he became deputy United States land surveyor and continued to serve in that capacity until his death in 1887. See Wilbur Fiske Stone, *History of Colorado*, 4 vols. (Chicago: S. J. Clarke Publishing Co., 1918), 2:614–16.

47
Bennet and some of the activities he describes are mentioned in Stanley W. Zamonski and Teddy Keller, *The Fifty-Niners: Roaring Denver in the Gold Rush Days* (Frederick, Colo.: Jende-Hagen Bookcorp, 1961), 145–59. Unfortunately this popular secondary source is not specifically documented.

48
McClure confronted many people, including Wynkoop, but probably would not have challenged him to a duel (Zamonski and Keller, *The Fifty-Niners*, 180).

49
There is no reference to Bennet in Zamonski and Keller's description of West's murder and subsequent events, including the day's delay in Young's hanging (ibid., 83–84).

50
In addition, Bennet helped draft a "constitution" for the "People's Government of the City of Denver." See Jerome C. Smiley, *History of Denver with Outlines of the Earlier History of the Rocky Mountain Country* (Denver: Denver Times/Times-Sun Publishing Co., 1901; Old Americana Publishing Co., 1978), 633.

51
"There happened to be in camp a copy of the 'Iowa Statutes;' these were followed. They were taken from the extensive law library of Judge Bennet, who, because of the size of his library, was regarded as the oracle of the country, he having by far the largest and most valuable collection, viz., fourteen volumes" (Peter Wikoff, "Bench and Bar of Denver and Colorado," *Magazine of Western History* 9 [March 1889]: 607).

52
The date of 1850, which appears on the transcript, is more than likely an error of transcription rather than a lapse of memory. Bennet, however, does confuse some minor dates here. The crime, not the trial, took place on November 30, 1860; the trial occurred on December 20; and Waters was sentenced at the trial to be executed on December 21. See *Rocky Mountain News*, December 26, 1860, p. 1.

53
The Hallett and Bennet partnership is discussed in John D. W. Guice, *The Rocky Mountain Bench: The Territorial Supreme Courts of Colorado, Montana, and Wyoming, 1861–1890* (New Haven: Yale University Press, 1972), 98.

54
The Cherry Creek flood occurred on May 19, 1864. See Albert B. Sanford, "The 'Big Flood' in Cherry Creek, 1864," *The Colorado Magazine* 4 (May 1927): 100–105.

55
Bennet is confused here both as to the chronology of events and the cause and effect relationship between the Confederate flag raising at Wallingford and Murphy's store (which he places in January 1861) and his own raising of the stars and stripes on February 22, Washington's Birthday. Bennet's flag-raising ceremony occurred first, while Confederate flag raising took place two months later, on April 24 (see *Rocky Mountain News*, February 22, 1861, p. 2, and April 25, p. 3). Hall, in his *History of the State of Colorado*, 1:270, makes the same error, as do Zamonski and Keller (*The Fifty-Niners*, 236–39), who compound the problem by misconstruing another patriotic Union celebration, held on the evening of April 25, as Bennet's. This second celebration and the resolution for Union support that came out of it is mentioned in the *Rocky Mountain News* of April 26, 1861, and recounted by LeRoy R. Hafen, who does not mention

Bennet's patriotic party (*Colorado and Its People: A Narrative and Topical History of the Centennial State*, 4 vols. [New York: Lewis Publishing Co., Inc., 1948], 1:279). Smiley, who cites Bennet as a source, places the events in their proper sequence (*History of Denver*, 376). Since the second Union demonstration followed directly on the heels of the Wallingford and Murphy affair, and since Bennet may have been present, he might easily have identified it in later years with his own flag raising party on Washington's Birthday two months earlier.

56
Gilpin's biographer lists the date of his arrival in Denver as May 27, 1861, when he was greeted by Bennet, who had been chosen as speaker for the occasion. See Thomas L. Karnes, *William Gilpin: Western Nationalist* (Austin: University of Texas Press, 1970), 257. Bennet's speech is also mentioned in Hafen, *Colorado and Its People* 1:281, and in Stone, *History of Colorado* 1:420.

57
Hafen states that Williams was defeated "largely because of his secessionist support" (*Colorado and Its People* 1:283).

58
Stone credits Bennet with preparing the bill and pushing it into law on April 21, 1862 (*History of Colorado* 1:394).

59
For details of Bennet's years as territorial delegate, see Jason H. Silverman, "Making Brick Out of Straw: Delegate Hiram P. Bennet," *The Colorado Magazine* 53 (Fall 1976): 309–27.

60
Lincoln's actual statement, made in his famous "House Divided" speech on June 16, 1858, was: "I believe this government cannot endure permanently half slave and half free."

61
An act was passed on March 3, 1863, to establish a branch mint in Nevada Territory. On December 10, 1863, Secretary of the Treasury Salmon P. Chase stated: "A report has been made on a site for a mint in Nevada and measures will be taken for its establishment as soon as possible." By June 1864 a joint resolution was passed to obtain title to certain property in Carson City. However, the 1864 annual report of the secretary states that a cloudy title to the proposed site of the branch mint prevented its establishment (*Congressional Globe*, appendix, 37th Cong., 3d sess., 1863, 221–22; ibid., appendix, 38th Cong., 1st sess., 1863, 9; ibid., 38th Cong., 1st sess., 1864, 3188; House Exec. Doc. No. 3, 38th Cong., 2d sess., 1864, 29).

62
For an account of the Holladay Overland Stage Line, see W. Turrentine Jackson, *Wells Fargo in Colorado Territory* (Denver: Colorado Historical Society, 11–13).

63
In the original typescript, this is spelled *Gos Utes.*

64
James Duane Doty, governor of Utah Territory, 1864–65.

65
Gordon Newell Mott, Nevada territorial delegate, 1863–64.

66
There was drought in California from 1862 to 1864. In 1863 San Francisco received relatively little rain from January to May and virtually none from June through October. It may have been as dusty as Bennet described. See Titus Fey Cronise, *The Natural Wealth of California* (San Francisco: H. H. Bancroft, 1868), 340.

67
Aaron Augustus Sargent, congressional representative from California, 1861–63.

68
While Grant did appoint Conner, no conversation with Bennet was recorded. See John Y. Simon, ed., *Papers of U. S. Grant,* vol. 13, November 16, 1864–February 20, 1865 (Carbondale: Southern Illinois University Press, 1985).

69
Lincoln's actual wording was: "With malice toward none; with charity for all; with firmness in the right, as God gives us to see the right."

70
Smiley (*History of Denver,* 418) describes an 1867–68 visit to Washington, D.C., by Carson, Bennet, Oakes, Head, Ouray, and "several other Ute chieftains."

71
This sentence originally appears in the transcript immediately following the discussion of the treaty with the Utes.

72
The sentence following this one in the transcript, removed because it bears no relationship to the previous subject, is: "In 1872 I was made president of the Society of Colorado Pioneers."

73
Apparently Bennet was in the beef business with George M. Chilcott in competition with McCook for Indian beef contracts. See Howard R. Lamar, *The Far Southwest, 1846–1912: A Territorial History* (New Haven: Yale University Press, 1966), 153, who quotes from the James B. Thompson Papers, Denver Public Library, Western History Department.

74
Hall, who referenced "furious assaults" on Bennet in the weekly *Mirror,* recorded Bennet's removal in 1874 (*History of Colorado* 2:158–59).

75
Although Bennet was involved in organizing the state government, he was not a member of the constitutional convention. Nevertheless, he did speak in favor of the constitution. See *Proceedings of the Constitutional Convention* (Denver: Smith Brooks Press, 1907), 15–17; Hall, *History of Colorado* 2:355.

76
Apparently Bennet served as a state senator, but only for one year, during which a bill was passed requiring that all doors in public buildings open outward. See *General Laws of the State of Colorado* (Denver: Tribune, 1877), 118–20.

77
"Swell top of a Saratoga trunk"—that is, a convex top.

78
The name of Defiance was changed to Glenwood Springs, and its first streets were named for Jim Blake, Isaac Cooper, Hiram P. Bennet, and Lottie Palmer. See Lena M. Urquhart, *Glenwood Springs: Spa in the Mountains,* 38–39; LeRoy R. Hafen, "Colorado Cities: Their Founding and the Origin of Their Names," *The Colorado Magazine* 9 (September 1932): 176; "Interesting Bits of History," *The Colorado Magazine* 23 (July 1946): 187.

79
Bennet no doubt meant sections 16 and 36, which were set aside for support of the schools. See *Statutes at Large of the United States from December 1873 to March 1875,* vol. 18, pt. 3 (Washington, D.C.: Government Printing Office, 1875), 474–76.

80
The position of state agent was created on March 31, 1885, and repealed April 10, 1891. There is evidence of various "acts making an appropriation" to pay Bennet over the years. The last, appearing in 1909, was labeled for the "relief" of Bennet and added "that the appropriation herein shall be in full settlement of all claims whatsoever of the said Hiram P. Bennet, against the State of Colorado under existing contracts." See *Mills'*

Annotated Statutes of the State of Colorado Embracing the General Statutes of 1883 (Denver: Mills, 1891), 2147–48; *Laws Passed at the Fifth Session of the General Assembly of the State of Colorado* (Denver: Collier and Cleaveland, 1885), 328–29; *Laws Passed at the Eighth Session of the General Assembly of the State of Colorado, Convened at Denver, on the Seventh Day of January, A.D. 1891* (Colorado Springs: Gazette Printing Co., 1891), 325; *Laws Passed at the Seventeenth Session of the General Assembly of the State of Colorado, Convened at Denver on the Sixth Day of January, A.D. 1909* (Denver: Smith-Brooks Printing Co., 1909), 49–50.

81
Bennet's role in establishing a local land office as territorial delegate may have led to his acquaintance with Louis Dugal, register of the U.S. Land Office in Denver and later a land attorney. Dugal prepared a detailed map of the city of Denver in 1868.

82
Bennet's difficulties with the state bureaucracy are borne out in entries and correspondence involving three governors and a variety of elected and appointed officials. He was authorized to receive $16,747.49 between 1891 and 1896. His 1888 contract did indeed call for 5 percent of school indemnity lands valued at $1.25 per acre. See *Executive Record* 5:66, 7:302, 7:333, 7:341, 7:367–68, and 9:548, Colorado State Archives, Denver; correspondence of Colorado Attorney General, Byron L. Carr, Letterpress Book 6:40–41, 7:152, Colorado State Archives.

INDEX

COLORADO HISTORICAL SOCIETY
BOARD OF DIRECTORS 1987-88

EDITORIAL REVIEW BOARD